Fear and Faith

edited by Rachael Kohn

The Bonhoeffer Legacy: An International Journal
Volume 7, Issue 1&2 2019

The Bonhoeffer Legacy: An International Journal is a fully refereed academic journal aimed principally at providing an outlet for an ever expanding Bonhoeffer scholarship in Australia, New Zealand and the South Pacific region, as well as being open to article submissions from Bonhoeffer scholars throughout the world. It also aims to elicit and encourage future and ongoing scholarship in the field. The focus of the journal, captured in the notion of 'Legacy', is on any aspect of Bonhoeffer's life, theology and political action that is relevant to his immense contribution to twentieth century events and scholarship. 'Legacy' can be understood as including those events and ideas that contributed to Bonhoeffer's own development, those that constituted his own context or those that have developed since his time as a result of his work. The editors encourage and welcome any scholarship that contributes to the journal's aims. The journal also has book reviews.

Business Manager

Mr Hilary Regan, Publisher, ATF Theology, PO Box 504 Hindmarsh, SA 5007, Australia.
Fax +61 8 82235643.

Subscription Rates

Print	On-line	Print and On-line
Aus $65 Individuals	Aus $55 individuals	Aus $75 individuals
Aus $90 Institutions	Aus $80 individuals	Aus $100 instiutions

The Bonhoeffer Legacy: An International Journal is published by ATF Theology an imprint of ATF (Australia) Ltd (ABN 90 116 359 963) and is published once a year.
ISSN 2202-9168

ISBN:	978-1-922582-43-0	soft
	978-1-922582-44-7	hard
	978-1-922582-45-4	epub
	978-1-922582-46-1	pdf

This periodical is indexed in the ATLA Religion Database® (ATLA RDB®), a product of the American Theological Library Association.
Email: atla@atla.com<mailto:atla@atla.com>, www: http://www.atla.com<http://www.atla.com/>.

www.atfpress.com

Fear and Faith

Christian, Jewish and Evolutionary Perspectives

edited by Rachael Kohn

ATF THEOLOGY

Adelaide
2019

Vol 7 No 1&2/2019

Contents

Bibliography

The Dietrich Bonhoeffer Works (English)

General Editors: Victoria Barnett, Wayne Whitson Floyd Jr., and Barbara Wojhoski.

Originally published in German as *Dietrich Bonhoeffer Werke*. Edited by Eberhard Bethge et al. Munich: Chr. Kaiser Verlag, 1986–1998.

DBWE 1 *Sanctorum Communio: A Theological Study of the Sociology of the Church*. Edited by Clifford J. Green. Translated by Reinhard Krauss and Nancy Lukens. Minneapolis: Fortress, 1998.

DBWE 2 *Act and Being: Transcendental Philosophy and Ontology in Systematic Theology*. Edited by Wayne Whitson Floyd, Jr. Translated by H. Martin Rumscheidt. Minneapolis: Fortress, 1998.

DBWE 3 *Creation and Fall: A Theological Exposition of Genesis 1–3*. Edited by John W. de Gruchy. Translated by Douglas Stephen Bax. Minneapolis: Fortress, 1997.

DBWE 4 *Discipleship*. Edited by Geffrey B. Kelly and John D. Godsey. Translated by Barbara Green and Reinhard Krauss. Minneapolis: Fortress, 2001.

DBWE 5 *Life Together; Prayerbook of the Bible*. Edited by Geffrey B. Kelly. Translated by Daniel W. Bloesch and James H. Burtness. Minneapolis: Fortress, 1996.

DBWE 6 *Ethics*. Edited by Clifford J. Green. Translated by Reinhard Krauss, Charles C. West and Douglas W. Stott. Minneapolis: Fortress, 2005.

DBWE 7	*Fiction from Tegel Prison*. Edited by Clifford Green. Translated by Nancy Lukens. Minneapolis: Fortress, 2000.
DBWE 8	*Letters and Papers from Prison*. Edited by John de Gruchy. Translated by Reinhard Krauss and Nancy Lukens.Minneapolis: Fortress, 2010.
DBWE 9	*The Young Bonhoeffer: 1918–1927*. Edited by Paul Duane Matheny, Clifford J. Green and Marshall D. Johnson. Translated by Mary C. Nebelsick and Douglas W. Stott. Minneapolis: Fortress, 2002.
DBWE 10	*Barcelona, Berlin, New York*. Edited by Clifford J. Green. Translated by Douglas W. Stott. Minneapolis: Fortress, 2008.
DBWE 11	*Ecumenical, Academic, and Pastoral Work: 1931–1932*. Edited by Victoria J. Barnett, Mark S. Brocker and Michael B. Lukens. Translated by Anne Schmidt-Lange, Isabel Best, Nicolas Humphrey, Marion Pauck and Douglas W. Stott. Minneapolis: Fortress, 2012.
DBWE 12	*Berlin: 1932–1933*. Edited by Larry L. Rasmussen. Translated by Isabel Best. Minneapolis: Fortress, 2009.
DBWE 13	*London: 1933–1935*. Edited by Keith W. Clements. Translated by Isabel Best. Minneapolis: Fortress, 2007.
DBWE 14	*Theological Education Finkenwalde: 1935–1937*. Edited by Victoria J. Barnett. Translated by Peter Frick. Minneapolis: Fortress, 2011.
DBWE 15	*Theological Education Underground: 1937–1940*. Edited by Victoria J. Barnett. Translated by Claudia D. Bergmann and Peter Frick. Minneapolis: Fortress, 2011.
DBWE 16	*Conspiracy and Imprisonment: 1940–1945*. Edited by Mark S. Brocker. Translated by Lisa E. Dahill. Minneapolis: Fortress, 2006.
DBWE 17	*Indexes and Supplementary Materials*. Edited by Victoria J. Barnett and Barbara Wojhoski. Minneapolis: Fortress, 2014.

Vol 7 No 1&2/2019

Editor's Introduction

Rachael Kohn

All go to God in their distress
Seek help and pray for bread and happiness
Deliverance from pain, guilt and death..
All do, Christians and others.[1]

This issue of *The Bonhoeffer Legacy* was prompted by the question how does one face the fear of death in a world beset with the COVID 19 pandemic that has already killed more than three million people and will assuredly claim many more before it is brought under control. For Dietrich Bonhoeffer, who faced his own imminent death at the hands of the Nazis, it is a given that his faith triumphed over his fear. Not in the way that he imagines in the reverent poem, The Death of Moses—magisterial, fulfilled and resigned to God's loving and just fate; but more like faith's struggle with the 'terrifying fear,' the 'sense that there is no way out' . . . 'of this hell of hopelessness,' in his sermon on Overcoming Fear. He describes this kind of fear, which is devoid of the power of faith, pitilessly as 'this person belongs to the devil.'

Fear is however an inescapable dimension of life and faith, and this issue considers how fear and faith are connected in Bonhoeffer's life and thought, in the biblical and rabbinic traditions of Judaism, in the challenging field of mission, and woven into our biological make up. To the extent that fear and faith also influence social and moral behaviour the final discussion extends to the realm of constitutional law in post-Weimar Germany.

1. Dietrich Bonhoeffer, 'Christians and Others' in *The Prison Poems of Dietrich Bonhoeffer: a new translation with commentary* by Edwin Robertson (Guildford, Surrey: Eagle Publishing 1998): 44.

When Bonhoeffer stated 'The Bible, the gospel, Christ, the church, the faith—all are one great battle cry against fear in the lives of human beings,'[2] he echoed many of the 150 Psalms which vividly describe God delivering his faithful from their travails: '*Cast your burden on the Lord, and he will sustain you, he will never permit the righteous to be moved.*' (56:22) Yet this easy faith that banishes fear is not always within one's grasp, nor was it always so for Bonhoeffer, for whom a true, active and effective faith was his life's project in words and in deeds.

Charles Ringma, whose deep familiarity with Bonhoeffer's writings resulted in the book of meditations, *Seize the Day with Dietrich Bonhoeffer* (2000), begins his essay, *In the World and Sore Afraid*, with a two-fold stated purpose: to humanise 'the hero' of Bonhoeffer and extract from his teaching and life the inspiration we need for our own time of crisis. Central to Bonhoeffer's Christ-centred faith was the call to live with 'large heartedness' helping others around him, even as he was vulnerable to melancholy and plagued by thoughts of his death. Ringma develops his insight into how Bonhoeffer's active commitment to change the Lutheran church, to renew its spiritual life and to reject its official Nazification required the faith-filled Christian to enter the secular sphere as Christ willingly entered the world in all its suffering.[3]

The missiological call to step into the world of suffering drew Michael Duncan to his first overseas posting in the slums of Manilla. In *Jesus is NOT all you Need in Overcoming Fear,* a graphically confronting account of his young family on their first venture into a faith-testing mission field, where the destitute live amid squalor, violence and death, Duncan discovers the redeeming value of friendship and community. In his fascinating analysis that looks at Soren Kierkegaard's influence on Bonhoeffer, Duncan compares the latter's 'catastrophising' of fear compared to Paul's 'normalising' of it, and finds a new way to speak about the intimacy and importance of friendship.

2. https://politicaltheology.com/overcoming-fear-sermon-dietrich-bonhoeffer/ Accessed 30 January 2021
3. Dietrich Bonhoeffer wrote in a letter, after writing the poem Christians and Others, 'It is not the religious act that makes the Christian, but the participation in the suffering of God in the world,' from *Letters and Poems from Prison*, p. 361, quoted in Robertson, *The Prison Poems of Dietrich Bonhoeffer*, p. 46.

Bonhoeffer's contrasting of fear and faith finds another test in two essays examining the Jewish understanding of fear and faith in the Hebrew Bible and rabbinic literature. In *When a Lion Roars, Who Can But Fear?*, biblical scholar, Martin Lockshin begins his discussion of fear by comparing New Testament with Hebrew Bible uses and finds many parallels as well as some differences. Danger, awe, and an ethical conscience all deploy the term *yir'at* (fear), and in a discussion brimming with biblical and rabbinic examples, Lockshin addresses the translation of the Hebrew term *yir'at* and compares its broader moral with its religious meaning. Lockshin shows that reverence for God and love of God are entwined in the Hebrew Bible and in rabbinic literature, with fear being understated, disarming the oft heard view that the Christian God is a God of Love while the Hebrew God is a God of Fear.

Alexander Green's focus on the medieval Jewish philosopher, Maimonides (1138–1204), examines the way he reconciled the biblical-rabbinic tradition's references to fear of the Lord (*yir'at Hashem*) or 'fear of heaven' (*yir'at shamayim*) with Aristotle's critique of fear. In *Fear and Awe in Maimonides' Thought*, Green explores the two distinct approaches to fear: pursuing knowledge leading to moral courage, and fostering an ethics of awe leading to acts of loving-kindness. In his systematic discussion, love and fear are compared while the fear of death is related to cowardice. Green's discussion of 'Moral and Political Courage' turns on an understanding of prophecy, while his consideration of 'Fear as Awe' brings into view Maimonides' comparison of the binding of Isaac with the story of the Garden of Eden, which pits the human intellect against the all-knowing God and ends in a lesson of pure humility. Like Ringma's essay seeking inspiration, Green's contribution points to the spiritual and moral foundations of active social justice.

So far, the discussion of fear and faith sits squarely in the received traditions of Judaism and Christianity, but with *Can Evolution Make Sense of Fear? Lessons from Darwin and Bonhoeffer*, we enter the burgeoning field of religion and evolution. Dominic Johnson, author of *God is Watching You: How the Fear of God Makes Us Human* (2016) teams up with Joseph Bulbulia, co-editor of the online journal, *Religion, Brain and Behaviour*, to examine the role that religion's supernatural punishment has in growing and maintaining more effective moral communities than other cultural groups. Taking as their starting point Darwin's observation that the visceral and emotional responses to fear are common to humans and animals, they arrive at a position where the automatic fear wired into our psyche can be supplemented or supplanted by awe, pointing to the 'evolutionary logic' of religion and its role in transforming humans into 'superco-operators.'

Finally, departing from the theme of fear, specialist in juristic thought and theology, Karola Radler brings us back to post-Weimar Germany, where Dietrich Bonhoeffer found himself in the maelstrom of the National Socialist regime's rewriting of the 1919 Weimar Constitution. It would do away with the Roman law (a 'Christian-Roman tradition'), and put in its place a system that 'destroyed the liberal basic freedoms' and replace the individual's sense of conscious free will with a law that demanded obedience to a totalitarian leadership. Radler's essay, which traverses the discussion that Bonhoeffer carried on in correspondence with Gerhard Leibholz, professor of constitutional law, is included in this special issue as a counterpoint to the discussions that have focused on fear and awe as an element in the individual's moral conscience, law abiding behaviour and community co-operation. In a sense, Radler's closely argued and highly technical essay demonstrates how far away the newly decreed German 'common law' was from the Jewish and Christian impetus to tie law-abiding behaviour to belief in a God, who stood above yet was inextricably invested in his people and the world.

Vol 7 No 1&2/2019

In the World and Sore Afraid: Dietrich Bonhoeffer and Living in Fearful Times

Charles Ringma

Introduction

There is little doubt that the COVID 19 pandemic is an event of monumental proportions. Virtually every country has been affected either directly or indirectly. Millions have fallen ill, many have died, health systems have been overwhelmed, and economies have been decimated.

This *is* a time of crisis. And crises are always unpredictable. We don't know when they will end. And we have no way of knowing what a post-pandemic world might look like. But we do need to be realistic enough to expect that in some countries this crisis will contribute to improvements in society, while in others, this pandemic has already led to oppressive government policies. But what is clear is that the poor and those with disabilities and mental health issues are greatly impacted by this pandemic.

Since this is not the first crisis to come our way, and there have been many crises in the past, we might learn something from our forebears who have lived in troubled times. One such person is Dietrich Bonhoeffer, the pastor/theologian/activist who lived during the Nazification of Germany and most of WWII.[1]

My intention in turning to Bonhoeffer is two-fold. First, I seek to humanise Bonhoeffer. Too often the heroes of history are made out to be more than human. This has also been true of Bonhoeffer. The

1. You may be interested to dip into some of the writings of Dietrich Bonhoeffer mentioned in this paper or you may like to meander with Bonhoeffer throughout the year in my *Seize the Day with Dietrich Bonhoeffer* (Carol Stream, IL: NavPress: 2000).

purpose in doing this is to make him more accessible to each one of us. Secondly, I seek to extract some salient concepts and strategies from Bonhoeffer's life and writings in *his* time of crisis in the hope that these may become sources of *inspiration* for us. The issue is not imitation, but gaining insight and encouragement.

But first, some comments about the title of this paper.

A Song of Realism and Vulnerability

It is well-known that not all those who have embraced the Christian faith are comfortable with the above title. There are those who do not see the importance of their situatedness and engagement with the world. Their orientation is escapist. They long for heaven. Theirs is a world-denying form of Christianity.[2]

While the above is the basic stance of some, this is all the more exacerbated in a time of crisis when we feel overwhelmed by society's issues and needs. In this setting it is easy to be nostalgic about the past and escapist regarding the future.

But as Niebuhr has pointed out, the Christian tradition has a more dominant motif than that of escapism. This is cast in a world-engagement and a world-transformative model. The church while living in the hope of God's final future, is to be an incarnational presence in the world. It partakes of the world's joys and sorrows. And its calling is to live the dangerous memories of early Christianity to the glory of God and for the world's well-being and shalom. Clearly, this was also Bonhoeffer's vision,[3] with his added orientation that it was only the suffering church that could be a blessing to the world. Bonhoeffer notes that 'the "must" of suffering applies to his disciples,' as much as it applies to Christ.[4]

The other part of the title is 'and sore afraid.'

2. See H Richard Niebuhr, *Christ and Culture* (New York: Harper & Row, 1975) where he discusses various ways in which the church has sought to relate to society.
3. Bonhoeffer thinks that the cultivation of a Christian inner life untouched by the world is 'tragicomical,' and that 'belonging wholly to Christ . . . [the Christian] stands at the same time wholly in the world', *Ethics,* translated by Neville Horton Smith (New York: Touchstone, 1995), 198.
4. Dietrich Bonhoeffer, *The Cost of Discipleship,* translated by R H Fuller (London: SCM Press, 1959).

One might well have expected a different title—'in the world, and not afraid.' This is a much more positive title. But this can so easily reflect an unhealthy triumphalism: 'Yes, so many are afraid at this time, but as a Christian I am not.' Not only is this unrealistic, it is also unhealthy. We should be afraid of this pandemic, and especially concerned about unhealthy long-term impacts it may have on our world. We can be sore afraid and still work for change, pray, and trust God to sustain and help us. Bonhoeffer from prison writes: 'we are only too familiar with life's anxieties,' but we can 'rise to the great demands,' but also to 'the tasks of daily life.'[5]

Finding Dietrich Bonhoeffer

We must not cast Bonhoeffer into the mould of a super-hero. Thus, we need to acknowledge his struggles,[6] and listen more carefully to his self-disclosures, even though in many ways Bonhoeffer was intensely private.[7]

But 'finding' Bonhoeffer is no easy task, despite the extensive nature of Bonhoeffer's own writings, the definitive biography by Eberhard Bethge,[8] and the extensive and ever-growing body of scholarship regarding Bonhoeffer.

The implications of this terse paragraph are myriad. First of all, there is the nature of Bonhoeffer's literary corpus. Due to his life's cir-

---

5. Dietrich Bonhoeffer, *Letters & Papers from Prison,* enlarged edition, edited by Eberhard Bethge (New York: Touchstone, 1997), 16, 217.
6. Towards the end of 1933 Bonhoeffer leaves Germany to serve two German speaking congregations in London, and in 1939 he leaves Germany to be safe in the USA. However, in both instances he realises his need to return in order to participate in the resistance. Bonhoeffer writes: 'I will have no right to participate in the reconstruction of Christian life in Germany after the war if I do not share the trials of this time with my people,' Edwin Robertson, *The Shame and the Sacrifice: The Life and Preaching of Dietrich Bonhoeffer* (London: Hodder & Stoughton, 1987), 172. And more poignantly in his prison writings, he speaks of being 'restless and longing and sick, like a bird in a cage,' and generalises 'we men of many scars,' Dietrich Bonhoeffer, *Letters & Papers from Prison*, 349, 351.
7. He writes: not everything should be expressed; 'many things in human life ought to remain covered.' And elsewhere: 'fright is surely something to be ashamed of,' and should only be expressed 'in the confessional,' *Letters & Papers from Prison,* 158, 146.
8. Eberhard Bethge, *Dietrich Bonhoeffer: A Biography,* revised edition (Minneapolis, MN: Fortress, 2000).

cumstances, Bonhoeffer's writings were 'incomplete, occasional, and fragmented'.[9] Most of his writings were 'essays, papers, and lectures prepared for specific occasions,' and his major work, *Ethics,* 'was never completed'.[10] The consequence of this is that it has placed Bonhoeffer in a 'kaleidoscope of interpretations'.[11] Second, because of the fragmentary nature of Bonhoeffer's writings, some scholars have taken different starting points in making sense of Bonhoeffer,[12] while others have sought to find a fundamental continuity in Bonhoeffer's writings. Some have seen this in terms of Bonhoeffer's Christology,[13] others in terms of his sociality,[14] and others in the three phases of Bonhoeffer's life—'discipleship and community,' 'involvement in the struggle for justice and peace', and 'faith in a secular age'.[15] Third, while appropriately impressed by Eberhard Bethge's monumental work on Bonhoeffer, we do need to ask whether he has contributed to a *particular* understanding of Bonhoeffer. Stephen Haynes, for example, is of the opinion that Bethge has contributed to seeing Bonhoeffer as 'Saint.'[16]

And finally, even though Bonhoeffer himself claims 'I don't think I've ever changed very much,'[17] one cannot but gain the impression that much changed for him in deciding to study theology, in his concern for socially disadvantaged youth, his very early critique of Hitler and his support of the Jews, his personal commitment to the Sermon on the Mount, his commitment to the church, his ecumenical endeavours, his communal formation of clergy, his involvement in the *Abwehr,* and his probing expressions about new understandings of Christianity in the post-war world.

---

9. Stephen R Haynes, *The Bonhoeffer Phenomenon: Portraits of a Protestant Saint* (Minneapolis, MN: 2004), 2.
10. John W de Gruchy, 'The Reception of Bonhoeffer's Theology', in *The Cambridge Companion to Dietrich Bonhoeffer,* edited by John W de Gruchy (Cambridge: Cambridge University Press, 1999), 94.
11. de Gruchy, 'The Reception of Bonhoeffer's Theology', 95.
12. Haynes notes that the more radical interpreters of Bonhoeffer 'read Bonhoeffer's prison writings without regard for the rest of his theological corpus', *The Bonhoeffer Phenomenon,* 22.
13. 'The Reception of Bonhoeffer's Theology', de Gruchy, 102.
14. Clifford J Green, *Bonhoeffer: A Theology of Sociality,* revised edition (Grand Rapids, MI: Eerdmans, 1999).
15. de Gruchy, 'The Reception of Bonhoeffer's Theology', 103.
16. Haynes, *The Bonhoeffer Phenomenon*, 147.
17. *Letters & Papers from Prison,* 275.

The above suggests a dynamic narrative. What makes this so challenging is the link in Bonhoeffer's life between thought (theology), deed (missional practices), and context (the response to Fascism and the realities of WWII). And this can readily take on mythic proportions: the god of evil, Hitler, and the almost solitary Bonhoeffer as the combatant 'in the service of Good'.[18] It should, therefore, not surprise us that Bonhoeffer can never be nicely placed in a particular box.[19] In fact, what one sees, is the relentless ever-bending of Bonhoeffer's life towards a faithful and costly following of Christ, and all the paradox and ambiguity that this brings. If Christ himself is the great enigmatic figure in history, then the faithful following of Christ can hardly issue as a life devoid of complexity and controversy.

The Vulnerable Bonhoeffer

Without in any way making light of the above complexities regarding Bonhoeffer, we want to probe the extent to which Bonhoeffer struggled with the issues of his life and thus gain a more realistic perspective. As we noted earlier, we need to be careful not to cast him as some super-hero, for if he was such, he would be of little help to us who are struggling in this present pandemic.

While we may be tempted to begin a reflection on this dimension of Bonhoeffer's life by starting with his sermon on fear,[20] or his acknowledgement that 'difficulties are magnified out of all proportion

18. Haynes, *The Bonhoeffer Phenomenon*, 5.

19. Haynes notes the 'bewildering plethora of interpretations,' and those who see Bonhoeffer as a 'champion of orthodoxy, neoorthodoxy, the theology of secularity, political and liberation theologies, religious pluralism, and postmodernism', 10. But we should not be too surprised about this diversity giving our comments in the above paragraph and the fact that we do access the 'other' in the light of our own concerns.

20. In an early sermon Bonhoeffer notes that loss, illness and loneliness, among many other factors, can spawn fear, and this 'takes away a person's humanity'. And that fear can conquer us to the point that 'we don't even want to find a way out.' He then gives that a probing contemporary grounding stating that fear is 'in Germany', 'in our own lives', and 'in the nave of this church'. His confidence in overcoming fear is not self-effort, but aligning oneself with a God who has embraced the cross. He concludes: 'there is no way to life for a Christian without being crucified', https://politicaltheology.com/overcoming-fear-sermon-dietrich-bonhoeffer/

. . . by fear and anxiety',[21] I wish to start elsewhere. The reason for this is that Bonhoeffer is not primarily moved by idealism, psychology, or pragmatism, but by a Christological centre.

Bonhoeffer develops this centre in ontological terms. He writes: 'Christ is his being, *pro me,*' and in freedom 'has bound his existence to me'.[22] Christ is thus with Bonhoeffer as 'brother' but also as 'the new creation'.[23] Bound to the One who has bound himself to Bonhoeffer, Dietrich is able to face his own issues and struggles and face the monumental challenges in his world.

That this faith dynamic does not lead to elitism or escapism is due to Bonhoeffer's formulation of his Christology. He writes: 'we have seen the exalted one, only as the crucified; the sinless one, only as the guilt-laden; the risen one, as the humiliated.' And he continues: 'even as the risen one he does not lift his incognito.'[24] Bonhoeffer concludes: 'it is with this humiliated one that the Church goes its own way of humiliation,' and in this way the people of faith are to live in 'the way of Christ.'[25]

Living out of this identificational centre, Bonhoeffer is able to acknowledge the reality of his life's circumstances—'human quality' is eroded and 'chaos is at the door'[26]—but we are called to 'large-heartedness' and 'sympathy' which 'grows in proportion to the fear of approaching disaster'.[27]

This way of living, Bonhoeffer asserts is not based on reason, impulsiveness, the solo effort, duty, and 'private virtuousness', but in 'responsible action in faith in exclusive allegiance to God'.[28] His profound concern is that many people have 'so little ground under their feet' in responding to life's difficulties.[29]

Bonhoeffer acknowledges his own struggles. He writes: 'we are only too familiar with life's anxieties and with all the other destructive effects of prolonged personal insecurity.'[30] In his poems, Bonhoeffer

21. *Letters & Papers from Prison,* 177.
22. Dietrich Bonhoeffer, *Christ the Center,* translated by Edwin H Robertson (New York: HarperSanFrancisco, 1978), 47, 48.
23. *Christ the Center,* 57.
24. *Christ the Center,* 112.
25. *Christ the Center,* 113.
26. *Letters & Papers from Prison,* 12.
27. *Letters & Papers from Prison,* 13.
28. *Letters & Papers from Prison,* 5.
29. *Letters & Papers from Prison,* 3.
30. *Letters & Papers from Prison,* 16

speaks of being 'restless and longing and sick, like a bird in a cage', of being a 'woebegone weakling', of being a person 'of many scars', and while 'defiant' also 'despondent' because 'one day turns into another / one that could have nothing new, nothing better'.[31]

In his letter to Eberhard Bethge who is deployed to military service, Bonhoeffer writes: that he is 'to meet an unknown future' about which 'one can do virtually nothing'.[32] Bonhoeffer continues: I 'have to try very hard not to let my thoughts dwell on the many cares and anxieties that beset you.'[33] And he has already acknowledged that in the present circumstances 'we feel that we really belong to death already'.[34]

But he makes it clear that we must not ignore the 'adversities' of life, but 'to face them deliberately'. And we can't be 'torn into fragments' by life's difficulties.[35]

Bonhoeffer concludes that the challenge is to live vicariously for 'the next generation' and for 'those who suffer' so that they may live 'without fear or anxiety.' As such, there is the call to 'have some share in Christ's large-heartedness', and to show solidarity and 'real sympathy that springs, not from fear, but from the liberating and redeeming love of Christ for all who suffer.'[36]

Eberhard Bethge, Bonhoeffer's confidant and biographer, has made the observation that from early in his life Bonhoeffer had a 'lifelong preoccupation with whether and how he would face up to death', and that the 'two companions whom he feared [were] *tristia* and *accidie*'.[37] Bethge continues that at the Finkenwalde seminary Bonhoeffer suffered from 'persistent melancholy', and that in prison Bonhoeffer resisted suicide 'because I am already basically dead'.[38] But even in these difficult prison circumstances, Bonhoeffer did much to help other prisoners, including referring the families of prisoners to make contact with his parents to obtain practical and legal help.[39]

31. *Letters & Papers from Prison*, 348, 351.
32. *Letters & Papers from Prison*, 190.
33. *Letters & Papers from Prison*, 198.
34. *Letters & Papers from Prison*, 16.
35. *Letters & Papers from Prison*, 159, 200.
36. *Letters & Papers from Prison*, 15–17, 14.
37. Bethge, *Dietrich Bonhoeffer: A Biography*, 38, 39.
38. Bethge, *Dietrich Bonhoeffer: A Biography*, 833, 832.
39. Bethge, *Dietrich Bonhoeffer: A Biography*, 849.

Bethge concludes that Bonhoeffer wrote prayers for his fellow prisoners, wrote a report to the prison superintendent regarding improving prison conditions, but like the other prisoners 'shared their anxieties, privations, and little joys'.[40]

Reading the Signs of the Times

Having seen something of Bonhoeffer's vulnerability, as well as his sustaining faith, we now turn to what we may learn from him as *inspiration* for the challenge we face in this time of crisis.

Hitler became Chancellor of Germany on 30 January, 1933 and on 1 February, 1933 Bonhoeffer gave a radio address where he attacked the concept of the leadership principle. This broadcast was shut down midway in its presentation. What this indicates is that Bonhoeffer, deeply shaped by the gospel and his theological formation, was able very early to discern perverted political concepts and to see something of their long-term consequences. This discernment was articulated in his Christology lectures at the University of Berlin in 1933 where Bonhoeffer expounded that Christ is not only head of the church, but also of nature and society.[41] It is therefore not surprising that Bonhoeffer was a strong supporter of the *Barmen Declaration* (1934) with its repudiation of the idea that the church should accept 'happenings and powers, images and truths as divine revelation alongside this one Word of God'. And that there are 'areas of our life in which we belong not to Jesus Christ but to another lord'.[42] In other words, God is Lord, and even the state does not have an arbitrary authority independent of God's mandate. All of this poses a challenge for us in our time of crisis. To be discerning, one needs to be formed by the gospel and one needs a theology that is world-engaging. Moreover, one needs to resist the temptation to look to other 'lords' for life's realities and meaning. And one needs to be willing to make a prophetic stand. The contemporary church in the West is not so strong in any of these important areas. And one wonders whether in the present coronavirus crisis, the community of faith and its leaders and people are

40. Bethge, *Dietrich Bonhoeffer: A Biography*, 850, 853.
41. Dietrich Bonhoeffer, *Christ the Center: A New Translation* (New York: HarperSanFrancisco, 1978).
42. *Creeds of the Churches*, edited John H Leith (New York: Anchor, 1963), 520.

discerning enough to see both the pitfalls and opportunities in this difficult time. Clearly, the church at this time cannot simply be concerned about its own well-being, but should be both a caring and prophetic community.

Practical Engagement

It is one thing to see when things are going bad, it is altogether something else to engage in creating an alternative. Bonhoeffer, along with others, was appalled at the Nazification of the Lutheran Church, and worked to create the Confessing Church as a movement opposed to the political 'takeover' of the state church. In this challenging endeavour Bonhoeffer engaged in training clergy for the Confessing Church through the use of Monastic practices rather than the more typical university setting. Something of the gestalt of this new way of clergy formation is told in his classic, *Life Together.*[43] The point here is that the circumstances of crises open doors to do things differently, and hopefully to do things better. This requires insight, creativity and courage. The important lesson for us is whether we will lapse back to the old normal or will we take this opportunity to deepen and strengthen the life of the church and make it more communal, formative and prophetic?

A Deeper Spirituality

Bonhoeffer was convinced that difficult times called for strengthening the spiritual life of members of the faith community. In his *The Cost of Discipleship*[44] he challenges the value for the Reign of God of a life built on 'cheap grace' which is 'grace without the cross.'[45] In contrast, Bonhoeffer proposes that grace is costly because it 'cost God the life of his Son,' and that 'grace and discipleship are inseparable'.[46] He goes on to suggest that discipleship 'binds them [Christians] to Jesus Christ alone,' and that this leads to a 'life of absolute insecurity'.[47]

43. Dietrich Bonhoeffer, *Life Together* (New York: HarperSanFrancisco 1954).
44. Dietrich Bonhoeffer, *The Cost of Discipleship* (London: SCM Press, 1959).
45. *The Cost of Discipleship*, 36.
46. *The Cost of Discipleship*, 37, 38.
47. *The Cost of Discipleship*, 53, 49.

Bonhoeffer continues: 'the "must" of suffering applies to his [Christ's] disciples' as much as it did to Christ himself.[48] In speaking about a deeper spirituality Bonhoeffer does not simply have in mind a self and inner focussed spirituality. He notes that Christians can't 'run away from the world and huddle together in a little band'.[49] Instead, just as Jesus 'suffered for the sake of all his people',[50] so Christian concern and love is for all humanity. Thus, Bonhoeffer asks: 'who will come forward to help him [Christ] and work with him'?[51] He concludes that in this way 'the Body of Christ makes a deep invasion into the sphere of secular life', and that the faith community seeks to do good 'without limit or reserve', whether 'the State be good or bad'.[52] The challenges here are multiple. But the core question is: what will it take for the contemporary church to be a community that forms its people into Christlikeness, spiritual practices, and costly engagement with the issues of our time?

Costly Identification and Suffering

Bonhoeffer's concept of following Christ in discipleship led him ever more deeply into offering resistance to Hitler's madness. In the midst of the suffering of the Jews, the closure of the seminary where Bonhoeffer taught, the weakness of the Confessing Church and the outbreak of WWII, Bonhoeffer had to face the question whether the Christian response was to pick up the bodies of those run over on the footpath by a madman or to wrest the wheel out of his hands.[53] Bonhoeffer wrestled with these and related issues in his *Ethics*,[54] and outworked this in his involvement with the *Abwehr* and their work of resistance to Hitler and their attempts to eradicate him. In engag-

48. *The Cost of Discipleship*, 77.
49. *The Cost of Discipleship*, 170–171.
50. *The Cost of Discipleship*, 179.
51. *The Cost of Discipleship*, 181.
52. *The Cost of Discipleship*, 241, 236, 237.
53. Renate Wind, *A Spoke in the Wheel: The Life of Dietrich Bonhoeffer* (London: SCM Press, 1991). See Bonhoeffer's statement whether one must consider to 'put a spoke in the wheel [of the state]', John A Moses, 'Bonhoeffer's Germany: The Political Context', in *The Cambridge Companion to Dietrich Bonhoeffer*, edited by John W de Gruchy (Cambridge: Cambridge University Press, 1999), 20.
54. Dietrich Bonhoeffer, *Ethics* (New York: Touchstone, 1995).

ing the complexity and dialectic of holiness in Christ and worldly engagement, Bonhoeffer formulated some core concepts. 1) While the 'Christian life is the dawning of the ultimate,' that is, 'the life of Jesus Christ in me',[55] and its fuller unveiling in God's final future, the Christian is called to live the life of faith in the here and the now. Bonhoeffer calls that living in the penultimate, that is, living in the now for the sake of the future. And that is messy, challenging and humbling. By way of example, Bonhoeffer refers to involvement in war. He holds that war is 'not arbitrarily killing' but this articulation absolves no one. All 'must share in bearing the consequences of collective guilt'[56] in relation to war. Basically, what Bonhoeffer is suggesting is that the Christian does not live in the world in an isolated holy cocoon, but is engaged and implicated in both the goodness and folly of social existence. And thus, none of us has clean hands.[57] 2) Bonhoeffer makes it clear that the 'ultimate . . . determines the penultimate', that is, the Kingdom of God and the Gospel determine how we are to act in the world, but 'the penultimate must be preserved', (that is, the ordinary realities of social life), for the sake of the ultimate.[58] And this 'throws' every Christian into the messiness and contradictions of life where one seeks to do God's good often in circumstances of compromise, failure and sin. 3) To this complexity Bonhoeffer adds the notion of *Stellvertreter*, the one who shares in other people's guilt.[59] Put most basically, Bonhoeffer believes that God in Christ stoops down into the 'depths of downfall, of guilt, and misery' of humanity,[60] and redemptively takes that upon himself. *Bonhoeffer goes on to suggest that Christians should do the same in taking upon themselves the folly and sins of others in 'redemptive' suffering.* He writes: the Christian also 'has to bear the sins of others' and bear 'their shame.'[61] What this means for Christians in the present pandemic is that they too can fall

55. Bonhoeffer, *Ethics*, 140, 141.
56. Bonhoeffer, *Ethics*, 158.
57. Bonhoeffer writes: 'we should not be surprised that 'the blood of martyrs will be required' in our day, but 'much of our own guilt will lie in our blood', quoted by F Burton Nelson, 'The Life of Dietrich Bonhoeffer', in de Gruchy, *The Cambridge Companion to Dietrich Bonhoeffer*, 45.
58. Bonhoeffer, *Ethics*, 133.
59. Christine Schliesser, *Everyone Who Acts Responsibly Becomes Guilty: The Concept of Accepting Guilt in Dietrich Bonhoeffer* (Germany: Neukircher, 2006).
60. *Ethics*, 136.
61. Bonhoeffer, *The Cost of Discipleship*, 80.

sick, they are to help others, they should influence government policy, they should participate in medical research, they should wrestle with what a post-pandemic world and church should look like. All of this is dealing with the penultimate. But they should also confess their failings and take upon themselves the shame of foolish policies in their respective countries. Thus, this time of crisis calls Christians not only to lament, but also to identificational suffering. While at the same time, Christians should be loyal to the way of Christ and his Lordship, and be willing to critique prophetically all attempts at creating other 'lords' who ask for our loyalty. Put simply and bluntly, Christ's lordship supersedes all national priorities and thus for the sake of the Kingdom of God we should become an 'enemy' of our country[62] when it perverts its rule and its commitment to justice.

What all of this suggests is that a crisis opens a wide window of grief and suffering but also provides space for a new imagination. Since crises have occurred again and again, we should learn from the past and some of its inspirational figures. Bonhoeffer is only one such a figure. You may be drawn to others. But do engage other figures and join the conversation. The present may present an opportunity to do many things better.

62. See William Stringfellow, *My People is the Enemy.* (New York: Holt, Rinehart, and Winston, 1964).

Vol 7 No 1&2/2019

Jesus is *NOT* All You Need in Overcoming Fear

Michael (Mick) Duncan

The traumatic culture change that saw my wife Ruby and I and our young family arriving in a Manilla slum as part of a missionary effort in the early 1980s[1] brought us face to face with fear and its many layers including those that hide in the guise of shadow virtues.

We had not begun to know fear until we relocated to the Philippines and incarnated into the heart of a slum. Our first day was unforgettable. We boarded a truck and were dropped off with our few bags, clutching our two-year-old daughter Emily and nine-month-old baby Thomas. The leaders of the Mission helped us unload and then drove off into the distance. As they did, we huddled together in the doorway and I began to cry. We were surrounded by thousands of extremely poor people whose language, culture and community we did not know. We had no idea where we would be sleeping, cooking or bathing. We had been left to figure everything out ourselves. It felt like we had been abandoned. As the night wore on Ruby dropped off into sleep out of bewilderment and exhaustion. I lay awake fearful of all the noises outside our thin walls, of the rats, spiders and cockroaches inside our plywood room. The sounds of machine gun bursts in the middle of the night were especially unsettling.

Within two weeks Ruby and I contracted a virus and were reduced to a delirious state. All Ruby could do was lie on her back and stare into space or sleep while I just managed enough energy to look after the little ones. We didn't know anyone, had no phone to call for help and simply had to ride it through. The only reprieve came when we

1. This story is told in my book: Michael Duncan, *Costly Mission: Following Jesus into Neighbourhoods Facing Poverty* (Melbourne: UNOH Publishers, 2007).

made our way to the Mission Retreat House for two nights and three days every fortnight for a team meeting. On that first retreat, as soon as we got through the high gate with our bags and kids, we dissolved into tears.

We had a violent wakeup call on our first Christmas Eve in the slums. Rocks were being thrown onto our flimsy roof in the dead of night. We huddled in a corner and prayed for protection. For years, we lived in a cockroach infested plywood shack with a mud floor covered in filth. The rats were as big as cats and at night they fought with snakes. In the first four years I got dengue fever several times and amoebic dysentery. We lost our third born child Joseph to a deadly virus. When I tell this story people ask, "Why did you do it? Why did you go?" In the next breath they suggest we must either be saints, very brave or have heard a booming voice from the heavens telling us to go. I gently inform them that none of the above fully explains our actions.

Our risky Asian venture, this daring act of discipleship, wasn't some sovereign act of God but *our decision* for God and the poor. We acted as free-will agents and decision makers. *We chose* between possibilities, *explored* the option of living in a slum, *decided* and then finally *stepped* out into the unknown with little or no 'guidance'. It was clear to us that Jesus needed some of his followers in the worst of places, so we simply put up our hands and said we'd go.

'Daring', 'venture', 'decision' and 'discipleship' are words employed by Dietrich Bonhoeffer to describe his own journey. He talks of the 'spirited deed'[2] and the 'free venture' that 'is not justified by any law.'[3] Bonhoeffer urges 'the free abandonment of knowledge of his [or her] own good' in the hope of performing 'the good of God.'[4] For such insights into what guided, motivated and kept him on track, we need only read his famous *Discipleship*.[5] Bonhoeffer was a keen reader of the Danish philosopher Soren Kierkegaard from which he may have borrowed some of his terminology. The following provocative lines from Kierkegaard are taken from *Provocations*:

---

2. Dietrich Bonhoeffer, *The Way to Freedom*, translated by Edwin H. Robertson & John Bowden (New York: Harper & Row, 1966), 110.
3. Dietrich Bonhoeffer, *Ethics*, translated by Richard Krauss, Charles C. West, and Douglas W. Scott, Volume 6 (Minneapolis: Fortress Press), 284.
4. Dietrich Bonhoeffer, *Ethics*, 284–5.
5. Dietrich Bonhoeffer, *Discipleship*, translated by Barbara Green and Reinhold Krauss DBWE, Volume 4 (Minneapolis: Fortress Press, 2003).

> It is dangerous business to arrive in eternity with possibilities that you have prevented from becoming actualities . . . Trusting in God, I have ventured, but I have failed—there is peace and rest and God's confidence in that. I have not ventured—it is an utterly unhappy thought, a torment for all eternity.
>
> A person can distress the spirit by venturing too much . . . But a person can also distress the spirit by venturing too little. Alas, but this comes home to him only after a long time, perhaps after many years when he is living in the security he sought by avoiding danger. Now he must experience the truth that he was untrue to himself. Perhaps it does not come until old age, perhaps not until eternity. In any case, the thing to do about venturing too little is to admit humbly before God that you are coddling yourself.
>
> We delude ourselves into thinking that to refrain from venturing is modesty, and that it must please God as humility. No, no! Not to venture means to make a fool of God—because all he is waiting for is that you go forth.[6]

On the idea of 'venture', Kierkegaard writes:

> A bold venture is not a high-flown phrase, not an exclamatory outburst, but arduous work. A bold venture, no matter how rash, is not a boisterous proclamation but a quiet dedication that receives nothing in advance but stakes everything.[7]

Such ventures are scary and can lead to fearfulness. Fear can arrest and disable us, staple our feet to the ground . . . stop us in our tracks. John Ortberg, in *If You Want To Walk on Water, Get Out of the Boat*, warns that fear can 'pull us away from the high adventure of extreme discipleship.'[8] In his sermon *Overcoming Fear*, Bonhoeffer describes how fear can wreak havoc in our lives:

---

6. *Provocations: Spiritual Writings of Kierkegaard*. Editor, Charles E. Moore (Farmington, PA: The Plough Publishing House, 2002), 396–400.
7. *Provocations: Spiritual Writings of Kierkegaard*, 398.
8. John Ortberg, *If You Want To Walk on Water, Get Out Of The Boat* (Grand Rapids: Zondervan, 2001), 17.

> Fear is, somehow or other, the archenemy itself. It crouches in people's hearts. It hollows out their insides, until their resistance and strength are spent and they suddenly break down. Fear secretly gnaws and eats away at all the ties that bind a person to God and to others, and when in a time of need that person reaches for those ties and clings to them, they break and the individual sinks back into himself or herself, helpless and despairing, while hell rejoices.[9]

Bonhoeffer lived in the shadow of fear but it has to be said that fear is an increasing reality for many of us in the twenty-first century. We see examples of terrorism regularly playing out on the evening news, new kinds of flesh eating bacteria are discovered in our hospitals; we are told an environmental apocalypse is imminent and of course there's a global pandemic, and with it the likelihood of financial collapse. We may be living in one of the most fear-filled times since Bonhoeffer faced his own conflicted challenges in the heart of Hitler's horrific attempt at empire dominance. Today, pervasive social media connects the world at light speed enabling a continual stream of bad news, speculation and rumour to feed our fear, uncertainty and doubt. It is estimated that one in five 18-35 year-olds around the globe identifies with feelings of anxiety.[10]

Theologians Scott Bader-Saye and Cornelius Plantinga, Jr., describe how fear can quickly sabotage people. In *Following Jesus in a Culture of Fear,*[11] Bader-Saye explains that a fear-filled society gives an excessive regard to what becomes an 'ethic of safety'[12]. This gives birth to 'three virtues' that of suspicion, pre-emption, and accumulation. Far from being virtuous, however these become 'splendid vices.'[13] While on the surface they may seem helpful cautions they are injurious to those who embrace them and are impacted by them. They pull us back from daring ventures and derail extreme discipleship.

9. Dietrich Bonhoeffer, "Overcoming Fear," in *The Collected Sermons of Dietrich Bonhoeffer*. Editor, Isabel Best (Minneapolis: Fortress Press, 2012).
10. *The Connected Generation*. A Barna Report produced in Partnership with World Vision. From 2019 onwards over 15,000 young adults between the ages of 18 and 35 in 25 countries and 9 languages were interviewed.
11. Scott Bader-Saye, *Following Jesus in a Culture of Fear* (Grand Rapids: Brazos Press, 2007).
12. Bader-Saye, *Following Jesus in a Culture of Fear*, 31.
13. Bader-Saye, *Following Jesus in a Culture of Fear*, 31.

We're so often told to be cautious, suspicious and keep our distance from strangers. Better safe than sorry, as the saying goes. When fear stalks the streets, such an approach is surely wise and to be commended? It's common sense. But what of the discipleship call to walk toward the stranger in our midst? What of hospitality? Bonhoeffer would join ranks with Rosario Butterfield who daringly reminds us that 'the gospel comes with a house key'.[14] Living in the slums was extremely hard for Ruby and I and our young family but later I discovered that inviting strangers to live in your home back in New Zealand was just as hard if not more so. Bonhoeffer, while in Berlin, opened his door to all manner of youth.

The second shadow virtue, 'preemption' includes fear of 'the other' and the temptation to control or get in first before they dictate the agenda. This pre-emptive behavior, notes Bader-Saye, can take the form of fight or flight.[15] We assert our boundaries and withdraw our presence when those boundaries have been crossed. This pushing and pulling is experienced by the other as emotional blackmail and therefore can inhibit the developing of 'meaningful and lasting relationships'[16] that are actually needed by strangers in our midst.

Living in a culture of fear also affects what we do with money. Of the third shadow virtue, 'accumulation', Bader-Saye writes:

> We fear losing our jobs. We fear that Social Security will not be there for us when we retire. We fear that our health-care benefits will not be sufficient to cover expensive treatments or long-term care in a nursing home. And so we come to believe that the more we have, the less we need to fear. We accumulate as an act of prudence, trying to secure ourselves against an uncertain future.[17]

Accumulation or saving for a rainy day may be prudent but can come at the cost of limiting or excluding our generosity toward 'the other'. In fact giving until it hurts might have the dual value of benefitting the recipient and breaking the hold that money has over us. Generos-

---

14. Rosaria Butterfield, *The Gospel Comes with a House Key* (Wheaton: Crossway, 2018).
15. Bader-Saye, *Following Jesus in a Culture of Fear*, 33.
16. Bader-Saye, *Following Jesus in a Culture of Fear*, 33.
17. Bader-Saye, *Following Jesus in a Culture of Fear*, 35.

ity rebounds and enacts a core principle of the Master. Once we see how this works out in practice it impacts other areas in life with the tendency to no longer base decisions around money but a deeper call to discipleship.

We can inadvertently use fear to shirk certain responsibilities; to avoid being hospitable, accommodating and generous and this can insidiously affect other areas of our life. Cornelius Plantinga, Jr. identifies conforming, conniving, leaving town, specialising, minimising, going limp, cocooning and amusing ourselves to death.[18] In a culture of fear we can so easily allow the majority to dictate our being and doing. Bonhoeffer dared to be different. To connive is to 'shut one's eyes to an injustice, to pretend ignorance of evil.'[19] This Bonhoeffer did not do. To leave town is 'going AWOL,'[20] to put yourself out of reach of what is happening. Arguably, Bonhoeffer did this a couple of times; especially fleeing to America at the very hour the Church in Germany needed him. He later acknowledged this mistake and returned to his ravaged land.

To specialize, is to give your life to a few things, especially in the face of a crisis. Again, Bonhoeffer chose a different path, that of giving himself to many things: becoming a chaplain at a community college, visiting the homes and families of boys attending his youth group, engaging in the church struggle, becoming a Pastor in London from where he maintained critical connections with church leaders in Europe and elsewhere. He lectured at the University, established a seminary, wrote books, mentored students and the list goes on. In the face of fear he lived an expansive life.

'Cocooning', in Plantinga's thinking, carries the idea of retreating 'into the small world defined by our friends, work, church, and family and build a snuggery there.'[21] Bonhoeffer remained alert to whoever was in front of him whether it was in the lecture room, church, neighbourhood, seminary or prison. Far from self-protecting himself in a small circle of family and friends he allowed his life and plans to be interrupted by so many. He took down the walls of his life and

18. Cornelius Plantinga, Jr. *Not the Way It's Supposed to Be: A Breviary of Sin* (Leicester: Apollos, 1995), 180–193.
19. Cornelius Plantinga, Jr., *Not the Way It's Supposed to Be*, 182.
20. Cornelius Plantinga, Jr., *Not the Way It's Supposed to Be*, 185.
21. Cornelius Plantinga, Jr., *Not the Way It's Supposed to Be*, 188.

allowed others to step into his space. As Miroslav Volf, might explain, his posture was one of embrace, not exclusion.[22]

Bonhoeffer, in his sermon on fear, asks, 'have you ever seen someone in the grip of fear?' Answering his own question, he writes:

> It's dreadful in a child, but even more dreadful in an adult: the staring eyes, the shivering like an animal, the pleading attempt to defend oneself. Fear takes away a person's humanity. This is not what the creature made by God looks like—this person belongs to the devil, this enslaved, broken-down, sick creature.[23]

With Bader-Saye and Plantinga, Bonhoeffer insists that a fear-filled person becomes a diminished person. Bonhoeffer continues, 'but the human being doesn't have to be afraid; we should not be afraid!' Is he right? And what of his solution to fear, which is soon to be described, is it helpful? It is to these questions that we turn to in our second section.

Part Two

Fear can sabotage, constrict and diminish a life. But to say, as Bonhoeffer initially did, that a fear-filled person 'belongs to the devil' and is a 'sick creature' is overly emotive and frankly inappropriate. Bonhoeffer delivered these words in 1933 in his mid-twenties. In this early stage of life he had just completed his academic work and traveled abroad. He hadn't yet faced the many obstacles, conflicts and dangers that would soon engulf his life. Harsh circumstances have a way of tempering and nuancing clever one-liners. Possibly, and without wanting to be unkind, such insensitive phrases might flow more easily at the back end of university and overseas travel for a young man struggling with ego and unbridled ambition?

In the second half of 1932 Bonhoeffer experienced a deep turning in his life. He came to see, in his own words, that he had 'plunged into work in a very unchristian way.'[24] In a letter to a former girlfriend he wrote of his ambition stating that he 'had turned the doctrine of

22. Miroslav Volf, *Exclusion & Embrace: A Theological Exploration of Identity, Otherness, and Reconciliation* (Nashville: Abingdon Press, 1996).
23. Dietrich Bonhoeffer, "Overcoming Fear".
24. Letter from Finkenwalde, 27 January 1936, Eberhard Bethge, *Dietrich Bonhoeffer: A Biography*. Revised Edition (Minneapolis: Fortress Press, 2000), 204.

Jesus Christ into something of personal advantage for myself.'[25] This co-opting of Jesus to achieve his own agenda, revealed a young man in need of open-heart surgery.

Bonhoeffer made a decision to break with his personal ambitions but transformation took time. He was still prone to making strident claims about those experiencing fear. Over the next two years he served up several more unhelpful phrases. Employing Matthew's account of Jesus sleeping while the disciples panicked and the boat was swamped with huge waves (Matthew 8:23-27), Bonhoeffer declared: 'fear is in the boat.' What is needed is for the disciples to see that 'Christ is in the boat.' He seems to suggest that in turbulent times we need only to see that Christ is in our boat, and then fear will 'shrink back.' He writes:

> So look to Christ when you are afraid, think of Christ, keep him before your eyes, call upon Christ and pray to him, believe that he is with you now . . . Then fear will grow pale and fade away, and you will be free, through your faith in our strong and living Savior, Jesus Christ.

But is this how the passage of Matthew works? Bonhoeffer is setting up an either/or between Christ and fear, as though the former makes the latter disappear. The text, however, is not setting up that equation. The word for afraid carries the idea of a person losing the moral gumption or fortitude needed to follow the Lord. Therefore, in the face of fear (not its absence), the disciples are to continue forthrightly following their Lord, who 'exercises a Lordship over absolutely everything.'[26] Fear in the boat co-exists with Christ in the boat. Fear is not the enemy that Bonhoeffer makes it be. This coheres with the life of the Apostle Paul who faced being banished, beaten, imprisoned and executed, challenges Bonhoeffer himself would soon face.

In Paul's opening chapters in his first letter to the Corinthians he writes of the centrality of Christ in his own life and for the Christians in Corinth. It is fair to say, Christ was definitely in Paul's boat. And yet Paul can also admit to experiencing fear and much trembling when he last visited these people (1 Corinthians 2:3). Elsewhere Paul talks

25. Letter from Finkenwalde, 27 January 1936, Eberhard Bethge, *Dietrich Bonhoeffer: A Biography*, 205.
26. Frederick Dale Bruner, *Matthew: Volume 1 The Christ Book Matthew 1-12* (Dallas: Word Publishing, 1987), 318.

about his visit to Macedonia, and being afflicted in every way—disputes without and 'fears within' (2 Corinthians 7:5). In other words, we see fear and Christ co-existing. It is in the face of fear that Paul acts forthrightly and follows his Lord.

While the early Bonhoeffer catastrophises fear, Paul normalises it. Fear is here to stay; it is the price of mission, part of the discipleship deal. What we need is a way to quieten our fears, which is not the same as getting rid of them or minimising them. Although Paul admits to 'fears within' he also highlights how he navigates that space. He talks of God consoling him. The word console can be rendered 'to comfort' which carries the idea of God coming alongside and being close and personal. How did this work out in Paul's case? Paul writes 'by the arrival of Titus . . .' (2 Corinthians 7:6). Paul still had fears but needed something else 'in his boat'. It was the gift of another person(s) that bought consolation in the face of fear.

Every two weeks while we were in the slums in Manila we would trek back to the Retreat Center of the organisation we were with and stay two nights and three days. Our lifesaver was to have others in the boat with us who were also living in the slums. We unashamedly had cry-time together. We ate, sang and enjoyed each other's company. While we can appreciate the popular worship song 'Jesus Is All I Need' and what it is trying to say, Paul; and us during our time in Manila, needed Jesus *and* people. Bonhoeffer came to the same conclusion in the five years after delivering his Overcoming Fear sermon. The disappointments were beginning to pile up in his life and fear was becoming a companion. In 1938 he published his *Life Together* in which he writes:

> The physical presence of other Christians is a source of incomparable joy and strength to the believer . . . The believer need not feel any shame when yearning for the physical presence of other Christians . . . The prisoner, the sick person, the Christian living in the diaspora recognizes in the nearness of a fellow Christian a physical sign of the gracious presence of the triune God . . . But if there is so much happiness and joy even in a single encounter of one Christian with another, what inexhaustible riches must invariably open up for those who by God's will are privileged to live in daily community life with other Christians![27]

---

27. Dietrich Bonhoeffer, *Life Together & Prayerbook of the Bible,* DBW Volume 5. Translated by Daniel W. Bloesch and James H. Burtness (Minneapolis: Fortress Press, 2005), 29.

One year before he wrote *Life Together* Bonhoeffer had been enjoying the privilege of living in daily community life with other Christians at the Seminary in Finkenwalde. He declares this community was a 'gift of grace from the kingdom of God.'[28]

The mature Bonhoeffer in 1944, writing to his beloved friend Eberhard Bethge from his prison cell, admits to a fear that is a daily accompaniment in his life.[29] In another letter he acknowledges to Eberhard that it is their friendship that gives him new courage.[30] The early Bonhoeffer talked of fear fading away, but the latter Bonhoeffer talks of fear as a daily companion. As Titus consoled Paul in the midst of fears, so Bonhoeffer found courage in Eberhard's friendship. And herein lies a more suitable pursuit for our fear-filled times, to recover the lost art and significance of friendships; to enter into committed relationships that are formed with sacred vows and solemn pledges one to the other.

In her award winning book *Confronting Christianity*, Rebecca McLaughlin cleverly writes:

> People sometimes say that the Bible condemns same-sex relationships. It does not. The Bible commands same-sex relationships at a level of intimacy that Christians seldom reach.[31]

McLaughlin is not talking about sexual intimacy but of same-sex friendships that reach levels of profound intimacy. Bonhoeffer and Bethge reached such a level. Charles Marsh in his famous biography of Bonhoeffer[32] paints a picture of two men, in a very intimate relationship. They share bank accounts, Christmas presents, bedrooms and holidays, spending constant time together and writing endearing letters to each other when apart. A preference for same-sex friend-

28. Bonhoeffer, *Life Together,* 30.
29. Letter to Eberhard Bethge 5 June 1944. Dietrich Bonhoeffer, *Letters and Papers from Prison,* The Enlarged Edition. Edited by Eberhard Bethge (London: SCM Press LTD, 1971), 319.
30. Letter to Renate and Eberhard Bethge 24 December 1943. *Letters and Papers from Prison,* 178.
31. Rebecca McLaughlin, *Confronting Christianity: 12 Hard Questions for the World's Largest Religion* (Wheaton: Crossway, 2019), 165 (Kindle).
32. Charles Marsh, *Strange Glory: A Life of Dietrich Bonhoeffer* (New York: Alfred A. Knopf, 2014).

ships was not uncommon, especially among intellectuals of the day. Wesley Hill calls such relationships Spiritual Friendships[33] where spiritual siblinghood is being experienced. This echoes the biblical mandate of being brothers in Christ. More than simply friendship, promise making and promise keeping mark this kind of relationship. It is a covenantal bond similar to those who are sisters in Christ. The same may be said for spiritual opposite-sex relationships with a brother or sister in Christ.

It is these intentional relationships that can embolden us to follow Jesus in a culture of fear. Jesus called his disciples friends, Titus encouraged Paul and Bonhoeffer enjoyed, and indeed relied upon, the deep bonds between him and Bethge. Ruby and I found courage to repeatedly return to our slum after our two night retreats, because we had been in the company of the committed. They were in the same boat as us. And yes, Jesus was also in the boat.

33. Wesley Hill, *Spiritual Friendships: Finding Love in the Church as a Celibate Gay Christian* (Michigan: BrazosPress, 2015).

Vol 7 No 1&2/2019

When a Lion Roars, Who Can but Fear?

Martin Lockshin

Some sources in the Hebrew Bible assert that belief in God removes fear, for example, 'The Lord is with me; I shall not fear'. Yet others encourage people 'to fear God' (using the same verb, although some scholars prefer translating the phrase 'to revere God'). This term, fear/reverence for God, both in the Bible and in later Jewish texts, is virtually a synonym for ethical behaviour and fear of sin. For example, when Joseph, in disguise as the vizier of Egypt, says to his brothers, 'This do, and live; for I fear God', he is referring to universal ethical norms, not trying to hint to them that he fears the God of Israel. Being conscious that God is watching and has the power to punish can deter people from unethical behaviour. Ultimately, classical Judaism urges people to live ethical lives using the same two-pronged approach as a modern government: educating its citizens to observe the laws because they are just, and at the same time employing fear by threatening punishment for infractions.

What do the Hebrew Bible and post-biblical Jewish texts teach about fear in general, and the fear of God in particular?

The Hebrew Bible and The New Testament

In a homily on Matthew 8:23–27, Dietrich Bonhoeffer describes movingly how fear can take over our lives. As a devout Christian, he solves the problem of fear though turning to Jesus.

> Jesus Christ . . . alone is Lord over fear; it knows him as its master; it gives way to him alone. So look to Christ when you are afraid, think of Christ, keep him before your eyes, call

> upon Christ and pray to him, believe that he is with you now, helping you . . . Then fear will grow pale and fade away, and you will be free.[1]

Other Christian scholars have argued that, in contrast to the New Testament, 'fear of God/YHWH' is 'the predominant trait in the personal relationship of Man with God in the Old Testament'.[2] Often this is the basis for contrasting the New Testament, where allegedly love is at the centre, with the allegedly more primitive fear-based theology of the Hebrew Bible.

As we shall see, fear plays a significant role in the Hebrew Bible. However, the supposed contrast between the Hebrew Bible and the New Testament is dubious for two reasons. The idea that hope in God and having a connection to God relieves fear is not an innovation of the New Testament; we find this message frequently in the Hebrew Bible, too (although naturally without the connection to Jesus). To cite a few of many examples: 'Though I walk through a valley of deepest darkness, I fear no harm, for You are with me'; 'In God I trust, I am not afraid'; 'When you lie down you will be unafraid. You will lie down and your sleep will be sweet. You will not fear sudden terror . . . For the Lord will be your trust'.[3] Second, the New Testament itself does not speak with one voice about whether fear is recommended. True, I John says unequivocally: 'There is no fear in love, but perfect love casts out fear. For fear has to do with punishment, and he who fears is not perfected in love'.[4] But Luke writes, 'His mercy is on those who fear Him from generation to generation', and, more forcefully, 'But I will warn you whom to fear: fear Him who, after He has killed, has power to cast into hell; yes, I tell you, fear Him!'[5] Paul also teaches: 'let us cleanse ourselves from every defilement of body and spirit, and make holiness perfect in the fear of God'.[6]

1. *The Collected Sermons of Dietrich Bonhoeffer*, edited by Isabel Best (Minneapolis: 1517 Media, 2012).
2. Walther Eichrodt, *Theology of the Old Testament*, volume 2 (London: SCM Press, 1967), 268.
3. Ps 23:4; Ps 56:12; Prov 3:24-26. Hebrew Bible passages are quoted from the New Jewish Publication Society translation (= NJPS), although I have made some minor adjustments.
4. 1 Jn 4:18. New Testament passages are quoted from the Revised Standard Version.
5. Lk 1:50 and 12:5.
6. 2 Cor 7:1.

Fear in the Hebrew Bible

Hundreds of times the Hebrew Bible addresses the basic emotion of fear.[7] Fear is not limited to humans; we share it with the animals.[8] People are often afraid with good cause. Being unafraid and simply trusting in a loving God when you are out of doors during a lightning storm is foolhardy.

In a passage explaining how prophecy works, Amos uses the inevitability of fear in certain circumstances to help us understand the overwhelming emotion a prophet feels when the Lord speaks:

> When a ram's horn is sounded in a town,
> Do the people not take alarm? . . .
> When a lion roars,
> Who can but fear?
> When the Lord God has spoken
> Who can but prophesy?[9]

Fear can be debilitating. When Deuteronomy details punishments that will befall the Israelites if they disobey God, it concludes ominously: 'You shall be afraid, night and day, with no assurance of survival'.[10]

But the Hebrew Bible does not have one consistent message about fear. The Babylonian Talmud notes that two biblical verses seem to contradict each other directly: 'Sinners in Zion are frightened' and 'Happy is the man who is always afraid'.[11]

Fear Leading to Inaction

A famous passage in the Babylonian Talmud explains the moral shortcomings and, particularly, the timid moral inaction that, according to the Talmud, led to the destruction of the second Temple in the year

---

7. Three separate roots meaning fear appear in biblical Hebrew: *y-r-'*, *h-r-d*, and *p-h-d*. They are generally synonymous.
8. See Gen 9:2, for example.
9. Amos 3:6–8.
10. Deut 28:66.
11. The Talmudic passage is in *Berakhot* 60a. The two biblical verses are Is 33:14 and Prov 28:14.

70 CE.[12] The Talmudic story is framed by the second verse quoted above, which reads in full, 'Happy is the man who is always afraid, but he who hardens his heart falls into misfortune'. Rabbinics scholar Jeffrey Rubenstein explains:

> The first half of the verse celebrates the God-fearing and cautious man. The second half conditions the promise of happiness with a significant reservation. Misfortune results when one 'hardens his heart' and refuses to act due to that fear . . . [The characters in the Talmudic story he is analyzing] were extremely cautious lest their actions be misconstrued . . . . They 'hardened their heart' by failing to take the necessary steps to save the community from its plight. The same fear of God that instills a sense of meekness, taken too far results in paralysis and misfortune, in the destruction of Jerusalem.[13]

In other words, the results of excessive fear can be devastating.

Fear and the Encounter With God

The Bible often refers to fear in the context of our relationship with God—both when God is the object of fear and when God relieves fear.

In biblical times, just like today, people fear what they cannot control and cannot understand. Surprising encounters with the divine caused many (but not all) people in biblical times to be full of awe, and even to fear that their lives were in danger. When Samson's future father, Manoah, realises that he had been talking with a divine being, he concludes, 'We shall surely die, for we have seen a divine being'.[14] Manoah's more insightful (and, perhaps, more divinely inspired) wife assures him that such fear is misplaced.[15] Still, Manoah is not alone in the Hebrew Bible. According to the book of Deuteronomy, immediately following the theophany at Mount Sinai, the Israelites en masse worried:

12. *Gittin* 55b–56a.
13. Jeffrey Rubenstein, '*Bavli Gittin* 55B–56B: An Aggadic Narrative in its Halakhic Context', in *Hebrew Studies*, 38 (1997): 28.
14. Jud 13:22.
15. Jud, verse 23.

> Let us not die, then, for this great fire will consume us; if we hear the voice of the Lord our God any longer, we shall die. For what mortal ever heard the voice of the living God speak out of the fire, as we did, and lived?[16]

The people wanted Moses to be the only one to have contact with God from then on,[17] in order to keep them away from the fearsome and ostensibly dangerous encounter with God.

Many more texts in the Hebrew Bible, though, develop the precisely opposite argument: God's presence is a reason **not** to be afraid. Isaiah is repeatedly reassured by God that he has no reason to be afraid, for example, 'Fear not, for I am with you'.[18] This identical thought and language appear also in earlier biblical books, for example when God tells Abram, after he won a battle but was concerned about a counter-attack, 'Fear not, Abram, I am a shield to you'.[19] When Jacob is fleeing from a brother who has threatened to kill him, God says, 'Fear not, for I am with you'.[20] In other words, we should resist the temptation to see a chronological development within the Hebrew Bible from early days when people saw the encounter with God as dangerous and frightening, toward later times when people saw it as a source of comfort.[21]

Desirable Fear of God

When the book of Exodus reports on the fear of the Israelites after the theophany at Mount Sinai, Moses says something apparently contradictory:

> Be not afraid; for God has come only in order to test you, and in order that the fear of Him may be ever with you, so that you do not go astray.[22]

16. Deut 5:22–23.
17. Deut verse 24.
18. Isa 43:5. This part of the book of Isaiah is understood to have been written by a relatively late prophet (sixth century BCE) whom scholars call Deutero-Isaiah.
19. Gen 15:1.
20. Gen 26:24.
21. On the variety of reactions to encounters with God in the Hebrew Bible, see James Kugel, *The Great Shift* (Boston: Houghton Mifflin Harcourt, 2017).
22. Exod 20:16.

Moses tells the people not to be afraid as a result of the encounter, and then says that the purpose of the encounter was to teach them to fear God! But what does 'fear of God' really mean for biblical authors?

When Abraham explains to Abimelech why he had used a subterfuge about the identity of his wife, Sarah, he says: 'I thought, surely there is no fear of God (*yir'at Elohim*) in this place, and they will kill me because of my wife'.[23] Abraham assumes that basic morality can be expected only from people who fear God (or perhaps the gods). Similarly, when Joseph, in disguise as the vizier of Egypt, says to his brothers, 'This do, and live; for I fear God',[24] he is referring to universal ethical norms, not trying to hint to them that he fears the God of Israel.

The Bible often portrays people as behaving properly due to their fear either of God or of God's representatives. When Joshua replaces Moses as leader of the Israelites, God ensures that he would have the basic prerequisite for a successful leader: 'On that day the Lord exalted Joshua in the sight of all Israel, so that they feared him all his days as they had feared Moses'.[25]

Fear of the Government

Such positive fear in Jewish writings is not directed only to God or legitimate religious leaders. Despite witnessing the Romans' destruction of the Second Temple and living under their cruel occupation, Rabbi Hananyah Segan ha-Kohanim, taught: 'Pray for the stability of the government; for were it not for the fear of its authority, people would swallow each other alive'.[26] Rabbi Hananyah's assumption is that even an oppressive despotic government is better than no government. A government with authority to punish motivates people to behave properly—or else.

Fear of the government and the courts continues to motivate people to be law-abiding today.

23. Gen 20:11.
24. Gen 42:18
25. Josh 4:14.
26. Mishnah *Avot* 3:2.

Fearing God = Observing Moral or Religious Law?

Commenting on a biblical verse that refers to fearing God, Bible scholar Jeffrey Tigay, who frequently prefers translating *y-r-'* as 'to revere', not 'to fear', explains:

> Reverence is man's response to God's power. It consists of both respect and awe at His grandeur and dread of His power, which serves as a deterrent to disobeying Him . . . Because of its deterrent effect, 'reverence for God' is virtually a synonym for ethical behaviour and fear of sin.[27]

In 2 Kings 17, King Sennacherib of Assyria destroys the Northern kingdom of Israel (c 722 BCE). The Assyrians, who commonly imposed population exchange when they conquered new territories, exiled the Israelites and 'brought [people] from Babylon, Cuthah, Avva, Hamath, and Sepharvaim, and settled them in the towns of Samaria in place of the Israelites'.[28] When these new immigrants encountered dangers that they could not cope with, they assumed, as most people in the ancient world would have, that the problem was that 'the nations [referring to themselves] which you [Sennacherib] deported and resettled in the towns of Samaria do not know the rules of the god of the land (*mishpat elohei ha-aretz*)'.[29] So Sennacherib sent to them an Israelite priest who had been deported, and requested that he 'teach them the practices of the god of the land'.[30] The Bible then reports: 'So one of the priests whom they had exiled from Samaria came and settled in Bethel; he taught them *eikh yire'u et YHWH*.'[31] Literally what the priest taught them was 'how to fear the Lord'. But modern translations understand, based on context, that the priest taught them 'how to **worship** or **obey** the Lord'.[32]

Here and in many other biblical passages, *yir'at YHWH* or *yir'at Elohim*, is best understood as synonymous with observing God's

27. Jeffrey Tigay, *The JPS Torah Commentary: Deuteronomy* (Philadelphia: Jewish Publication Society, 1996), 46–47, commenting on Deut 4:10.
28. 2 Kings 17:24.
29. 2 Kings 17:26.
30. 2 Kings 17:27.
31. 2 Kings 17:28.
32. See the translations of NJPS, RSV and NIV. *Cf* King James Version: 'and taught them how they should fear the Lord'.

laws, both the ethical and the religious. After Abraham shows his willingness to follow God's commands, even in the ultimate test of the binding of Isaac, God tells him, 'now I know that you fear God, since you have not withheld your son, your favoured one, from Me'.[33] The author of Qohelet (= Ecclesiastes), sums up the lesson that readers should take from his unusually pessimistic book: 'The sum of the matter, when all is said and done: Fear (*yera'*) God and observe His commandments. For this is the whole duty of people'.[34]

What does 'fearing God' mean in Qohelet? Consider this passage earlier in the book:

> Don't overdo goodness and don't act the wise man to excess, or you may be dumfounded. Don't overdo wickedness and don't be a fool, or you may die before your time. It is best that you grasp the one without letting go of the other, for one who fears God (*yerei Elohim*) will do his duty by both.[35]

For Qohelet, God-fearers are not paralyzed by fear of punishment, submitting to God's laws to save their skins. Rather, once again, fearing God is simply a synonym for observing God's laws.

Accordingly, many modern translators do not translate *y-r-'* as meaning 'fear' when it refers to God. For example, Qohelet's summary statement, as it appears in the New Jewish Publication Society translation, reads 'The sum of the matter, when all is said and done: Revere (*yera'*) God and observe His commandments.' When Isaiah, speaking in God's name, chastises his contemporaries for their religious nonchalance, he says, 'That people has approached [Me] with its mouth and honoured Me with its lips, but has kept its heart far from Me, and *yir'atam* of Me has been a commandment of men, learned by rote'.[36] It makes little sense to translate this last phrase literally as 'their fear of Me has been . . . a commandment learned by rote'. What Isaiah means is correctly captured by NJPS: 'its *worship* of Me has been a commandment . . . learned by rote'. Isaiah is not chastising Israelites who have a deep-seated fear of God. To the contrary—he is saying that although they observe the laws, they have no emotional or spiritual component to their commitment.

33. Gen 22:12.
34. Eccl 12:13 (my translation).
35. Eccl 7:16–18.
36. Is 29:13.

In the Hebrew Bible, fear or reverence for God is compatible with love of God. For example:

> And now, O Israel, what does the Lord your God demand of you? Only this: **to fear** the Lord your God, to walk only in His paths, **to love** Him, and to serve the Lord your God with all your heart and soul, keeping the Lord's commandments and laws, which I enjoin upon you today, for your good.[37]

Fearing God as a Motive for Behaving Morally

According to Jewish tradition, the Torah (or Pentateuch) contains 613 commandments, or obligations. Several medieval scholars wrote books enumerating and explaining them. These scholars listed both 'loving God' and 'fearing God' as obligations for the religious Jew.[38] But in the Torah itself, fear of God is often not invoked as an independent requirement, but as the reason to observe another commandment. Five times in Leviticus, fear of God is given as the reason for observing a specific law—always a moral law, regulating our behaviour towards other human beings.

The most famous one is 'You shall not curse the deaf, or place a stumbling block before the blind. You shall fear your God: I am the Lord'.[39] (The others are: showing deference to the elderly; not cheating someone when buying or selling merchandise; not exacting interest from someone in financial straits; and not working a labourer ruthlessly.[40]) Despite its strong emphasis on cultic laws, Leviticus never attaches the exhortation, 'You shall fear your God', to a ritual obligation.

The most famous Jewish Bible commentator, Rashi (Solomon son of Isaac, Northern France; 1040-1105) comments:

37. Deut 10:12–13. Emphasis added.
38. Moses Maimonides, *The Book of Commandments*, number 3 (love of God) and number 4 (fear of God); Moses of Coucy, *Sefer Mitzvot Gadol*, number 3 (love of God) and number 4 (fear of God); *Sefer ha-hinukh*, author unknown, number 418 (love of God) and number 432 (fear of God).
39. Lev 19:14.
40. Lev 19:32, 25:17, 25:36, and 25:43, respectively.

> For actions where only those who do them know their own motive, and others cannot know, Scripture states, 'You shall fear your God'.[41]

In other words, when you put a stumbling block before a blind person, it's hard to prove that tripping the blind person was your intention; even if there were onlookers, they could not know for sure. But remember that God knows your intentions.

Rabbi Moses Nahmanides (1194–1270; Spain and the Land of Israel) gives a slightly different interpretation:

> The verse warns about the most commonly occurring infractions.[42] People who curse the deaf and put stumbling blocks before the blind assume that deaf and blind people will never know about it. Accordingly [the Torah writes:] 'You shall fear your God', for God knows all hidden things.[43]

In other words, the Bible recognises that being concerned about what other people think, or about being punished, is often what keeps people honest. But how do you motivate people to behave properly when no one will know what they did? Leviticus answers: 'You shall fear your God.' If you fear God, you have a stronger and wider incentive for behaving morally.

The medieval Jewish Bible commentator, Rashbam (Rabbi Samuel ben Meir; Northern France c 1080–c 1160), expanded on this idea.

41. Rashi's commentary to Lev 19:14. On Rashi's commentary, see Eric Lawee, *Rashi's Commentary on the Torah: Canonization and Resistance in the Reception of a Jewish Classic* (New York: Oxford University Press, 2019).
42. In other words, although it is forbidden to curse anyone or to put a stumbling block before anyone, the verse chooses these example since they are more likely to occur.
43. Nahmanides' commentary to Lev 19:14. The sentences quoted were not part of the first edition of Nahmanides' commentary, written in Spain. He added them only after he moved to the Land of Israel, later in life. See Yosef Ofer and Jonathan Jacobs, *Nahmanides' Torah Commentary Addenda Written in the Land of Israel* [Heb.] (Jerusalem: World Union of Jewish Studies, 2013), 380–381. The same idea as Nahmanides' is found in Baruch Levine, *The JPS Torah Commentary: Leviticus* (Philadelphia: Jewish Publication Society, 1989), 128, 'This admonition seems especially appropriate for offenses that cannot be detected and that, therefore, are readily concealed. The deaf cannot hear what is being said about them, and the blind cannot see who causes them to stumble. But God sees and hears on their behalf and will punish their tormentors'.

An idiosyncratic list of offenders whom God will curse appears in Deuteronomy 27: people who make a sculptured or molten image . . . and set it up in secret; people who curse their parents; people who move a border marker between their property and that of their neighbour; people who misdirect a blind person; people who subvert the rights of the stranger, orphan or widow; a man who has intercourse with his father's wife; a person who has intercourse with an animal; a man who has intercourse with his sister; a man who has intercourse with his mother-in-law; a person who strikes someone else in secret; a person who accepts a bribe.[44] This list does not represent the worst crimes possible–neither murder nor adultery is included. None of these crimes, with the exception of fashioning an idol, is a religious infraction. Rashbam explains:

> All of them are [curses for] the type of infractions that are normally done in private, as I shall explain. There are two exceptions—idolatry and assault—which are normally done either in private or in public, and for that reason the text specifies [in those two cases that a curse is being invoked only on people who break those rules] 'in secret.' These verses do not invoke curses on [people who commit] infractions openly. Courts of law punish people for those 'overt acts,' as it is written at the end of all the curses (Deut 29:28): 'The concealed acts are for the Lord our God' [to take care of]; He will take vengeance on [people who commit infractions that are] 'concealed acts,' for they were cursed [here] in the name of God. But with 'the overt acts it is for us and for our children ever to apply all the provisions of this Torah.'[45]

Rashbam states that the Torah understands that proper religious and ethical behaviour generally result from our fear of the judicial system. Our fear of God should prevent us from committing the infractions that cannot easily be brought before a human court.

A vignette in the Babylonian Talmud illustrates this idea. Rabban Yohanan ben Zakkai, the rabbi who is seen as primarily responsible

44. Deut 27:15–25.

45. *Rashbam's Commentary to Deuteronomy: An Annotated Translation*, edited and translated by Martin Lockshin (Providence: Brown Jewish Studies, 2004), 153–154. In the continuation of his comment Rashbam explains how each of these infractions can easily be done without witnesses.

for helping Judaism survive the destruction of the Second Temple, was on his death bed. His students visited him, and asked for a final blessing. He said: 'May you have as much fear of God as you have of human beings'. The students responded: 'That's all?' [In other words, should we not be fearing God more than we fear human beings?] He answered: 'If only! [In other words, if only people feared God as much as they feared other people!] For when people sin, they say, "I hope no one saw me"'.[46]

Fear and Love in the Babylonian Talmud

In the vast corpus of rabbinic texts that have survived from Talmudic times (i.e. the first five centuries of the Common Era) we find a variety of voices. It is not always easy to sum up what the Talmud teaches about any topic, including fear of God.

As we have noted, in the Hebrew Bible fearing and loving God are not seen as contradictory; the requirement to do both even appears in the same verse.[47] In some texts from Talmudic times this approach persists. We just encountered Rabban Yohanan ben Zakkai's deathbed blessing to his disciples, that they should fear God as much as they fear people. The fourth-century rabbi, Rava, told two of his star students that while one of them operated on the basis of fear and the other on the basis of love, they were both 'entirely righteous'.[48] In a famous rabbinic text, Rabbi Hanina (second century) taught that 'All is in the hands of heaven, except for the fear of heaven', essentially arguing that human free will consists of the decision of whether or not we will fear God.[49] The contemporary scholar of Jewish philosophy, Zev Warren Harvey, places the statement against the background of Stoicism. 'The Stoics taught that all is determined except *ataraxia* [tranquility: ML] or *autarkia* [self-sufficiency: ML], and these traits are attained by freeing oneself from *fear of the gods*. Rabbi Hanina may be responding to the Stoics: determinism is overcome not by rejecting the fear of Heaven, but by embracing it'.[50]

---

46. Babylonian Talmud *Berakhot* 28b.
47. Deut 10:12.
48. Babylonian Talmud *Sotah* 31a.
49. Babylonian Talmud *Berakhot* 33b.
50. Zev Warren Harvey, '*Yirat Shamayim* in Jewish Thought', in Marc Stern editor, *Yirat Shamayim: The Awe, Reverence and Fear of God* (New York: Yeshiva University Press, 2008), 1–26.

But a minority of voices in Talmudic literature posit a hierarchy between love and fear. Rabbi Simeon ben Eliezer (second century) teaches: 'One who serves God out of love is greater than one who serves God out of fear'.[51] The midrash collection *Sifri* (c. third century) highlights the possible tension between love and fear of God:

> 'And you shall love the Lord your God' (Deuteronomy 6:5): Act out of love. The biblical text makes a distinction between acting out of love and acting out of fear. When people act out of love, their reward is doubled and redoubled . . .. You may fear your friend, but if your friend asks too much of you, you might leave the friend. Instead, you should act out of love.[52]

Rabbi Simeon prefers the service of God to be based on love. Fear might prove insufficient at some point. But the text of *Sifri* continues:

> There can be no love in the place of fear, and no fear in the place of love, except towards the Blessed Holy One.[53]

Ultimately, this text concludes that even though love and fear seem contradictory, and even though some, like Rabbi Simeon, see love as preferable, love and fear can coexist in the special case of a relationship with God.

Some classical rabbis see the fact that the biblical character Job is described as 'fearing God'[54] as a subtle criticism, implying that he did not love God.[55] But others disagree: just as the Bible describes Abraham as fearing God and also as loving God,[56] so also the reference to Job's fear of God should not be seen as criticism.[57]

Fear and Love in Maimonides

In medieval times, some Jewish thinkers wrote disparagingly about the idea of using fear of God to motivate people. The most famous

51. Babylonian Talmud *Sotah,* 31a.
52. *Sifri* Deut 32, commenting on Deut 6:5 and 10:20.
53. *Sifri, ibid.*
54. Job 1:1.
55. Babylonian Talmud *Sotah* 27b.
56. Gen 22:12 and Is 41:8, respectively.
57. Babylonian Talmud, *ibid.*

was Moses Maimonides (Spain and Egypt; 1138–1204), perhaps the central Jewish thinker of the Middle Ages. Maimonides criticised worship of God based on fear: 'It is not right to serve God after this fashion, for whoever does so, serves God out of fear. This is not the standard set by the prophets and sages'. With the misogyny typical of a medieval philosopher, Maimonides continues: 'Those who may serve God in this way are illiterate, women, and children, whom one trains to serve out of fear, until their knowledge increases and then they will serve out of love'. Serving out of love for Maimonides means that 'a person does what is truly right because it is truly right. This standard is indeed a very high one; not even every sage has attained it . . . A person who loves God with the correct love will straightaway observe all the commandments out of love'.[58]

But even Maimonides cannot imagine the Jewish religion without fear, as he shows in other writings. He was one of the medieval scholars mentioned above who, in his catalogue of the 613 commandments, listed 'fear of God' as a biblical 'commandment' obligatory on all Jews.

In his major philosophical work, *Guide of the Perplexed*, he writes that 'the final end of the whole of the Torah, including its commandments, prohibitions, promises and narratives, is one thing only—namely fear of Him [= God], may He be exalted'.[59] And in his code of Jewish law, he writes:

> It is our duty to love and fear this God . . . And what is the way that will lead to this love and fear? Contemplating His great and wondrous works and creatures . . . will straightaway lead to loving Him . . . And when he ponders these matters, he will recoil frightened, realizing that he is small, lowly and obscure, endowed with slight and slender intelligence, standing in the presence of Him who is perfect in knowledge.[60]

58. *Mishneh Torah*, Laws of Repentance 10:1–2.
59. *Guide of the Perplexed* 3:26, in the edition translated by Shlomo Pines (Chicago: University of Chicago Press, 1963), 501.
60. *Mishneh Torah*, Basic Principles of the Torah 2:1–2. Harmonising Maimonides' apparently contradictory approach to fear of God is beyond the scope of this paper.

Fear of God in Jewish Liturgy

The prayer book (*siddur*) is often seen as a handbook for what Jews should believe. Developed over centuries, its core, aside from the many citations from the Hebrew Bible, probably dates from the classical rabbinic period.[61] In the prayer book, *yir'at shamayim*, the fear of heaven, is seen as central. To cite just three examples from the daily liturgy: 'A person should always be God-fearing, privately and publicly'; 'Unite our hearts to love and fear Your name, so that we may never be ashamed'; and 'May He open our heart to His Torah, imbuing our heart with love and fear of Him, that we may do His will and serve Him with a perfect heart'.[62] (Note that here, too, in the liturgy, love and fear are seen as complementary.) Referring to a person as a 'God-fearer' (*yerei shamayim*) continues to be a serious compliment in contemporary religious Jewish circles. The scholar of Jewish education and philosophy, Michael Rosenak (d. 2013), describes the fear of God as 'the basic value term in the Jewish *paideia*'. It is 'the dominant end-aim of rabbinic educational reflection' and the 'high road to the palace of ideal human existence and self-realization'.[63]

Conclusions

This essay began with Dietrich Bonhoeffer's moving words that faith can remove fear from your life. Other Christian thinkers phrase their approach to fear differently. For example, the Rev Dr Rob Schenck, president of the Dietrich Bonhoeffer Institute, in Washington, DC, argues that Jesus taught that fear must be directed only to God. 'Learning to fear God alone will ultimately fill the anxiety space we

---

61. On Jewish liturgy, see, for example, Ismar Elbogen, *Jewish Liturgy: A Comprehensive History*, translated by Raymond Scheindlin (Philadelphia: Jewish Publication Society, 1993).
62. *The Koren Siddur*, with Introductions, Translations and Commentaries by Rabbi Sir Jonathan Sacks (Jerusalem: Koren, 2009), 34, 96, and 176. In the second passage, Rabbi Sacks writes 'revere' instead of 'fear', and in the third passage 'awe' instead of 'fear', for forms of the root *y-r-'*. In many old manuscripts of the *siddur*, the first quotation reads, 'A person should always be God-fearing privately', without the words 'and publicly'.
63. Michael Rosenak, *Roads to the Palace: Jewish Texts and Teaching* (Providence, RI: Berghahn, 1993), 86–87, 96, 110 and 144.

have in our lives with His peace. God is too big and too great to share that space with anyone or anything else'.[64]

Many of the Jewish texts seen in this essay offer a different approach, one that does not see fear as the enemy to be vanquished. With very few exceptions, Jews from biblical times to today have believed that fear of God was a good way to motivate people to behave properly. But other forms of human fear are also seen as having value. Just as we all obey the laws of our land both because we fear the sanctions of the government and because, ideally, we honour laws that represent the will of the people, so the religious Jew observes God's law out of fear of God and out of love of God.

In our perplexed world, we are told that following certain rules can help control a frightening pandemic. In this atmosphere, we carefully note how others behave. Some follow the rules because they are concerned altruistically about hurting others and/or because they believe that following the laws of the land is the right thing to do. Others do so because they fear for their own lives. And in most countries, many who behave properly fear the governmental sanctions, sometimes draconian ones, against those who transgress laws meant to protect public health.[65]

Ideally, everyone should behave properly on principle, or because they are committed to loving God or loving their neighbour.[66] But I know of no society that has ever succeeded in achieving that goal. Some forms of fear—of disgrace, punishment, or God's disapproval—have, at least since the days of the Hebrew Bible, been at the basis of all ethical communities.

64. https://tdbi.org/devotionals/what-to-do-with-our-fears/. Accessed October 19 2020.
65. For example, in Canada, people who enter the country and do not quarantine themselves can, even if they are entirely healthy and symptom free, be fined up to $750,000 CDN <https://www.canada.ca/en/public-health/news/2020/03/new-order-makes-self-isolation-mandatory-for-individuals-entering-canada.html>. Accessed October 19 2020.
66. A Hebrew Bible concept; see Lev 19:18.

Vol 7 No 1&2/2019

Fear and Awe in Maimonides' Thought[1]

Alexander Green

Fear is a basic human emotion common to all people. Yet, despite the distressing aspects of fear, Dietrich Bonhoeffer takes a remarkably hopeful approach to it. In his sermon, 'Overcoming Fear,' he states that what differentiates human beings from all other creatures is the ability to overcome fear, and he emphasizes that faith is 'a great battle cry' against it. But how do we understand fear? And is it something we can truly control and overcome? If one looks back to the ancient sources, one discovers that Aristotle and the Bible present different answers to the question of how to best overcome human fear. According to Aristotle in the *Rhetoric*, fear is 'a sort of pain or agitation derived from the imagination of a future destructive or painful evil'.[2] He implies that there is no universal list of fears that we all share, but that fear derives from a subjective perception of danger. It varies depending on when and how we perceive that this danger will bring harm to us. Aristotle also asserts in the *Nicomachean Ethics* that fear is a vice and not a virtue. The proper moral virtue is courage, which is the balance between the extremes of fear and confidence, or knowing when to be fearful and when to be confident.[3] However, in contrast to Aristotle, the Biblical and Rabbinic traditions seem to regard a certain type of fear—the fear of God—as the highest model for human conduct. As such, one finds statements in Biblical wisdom literature,

1. This article is a further development of my earlier article, Alexander Green, "Maimonides on Courage," *Jewish Studies Quarterly*, 22/2 (2015): 162–183.
2. Aristotle, *On Rhetoric*, trans. George A. Kennedy (Oxford: Oxford University Press, 1991), 139 (2.5.1).
3. Aristotle, *Nicomachean Ethics*, translated by Robert C Bartlett and Susan D Collins (Chicago: University of Chicago Press, 2011), 54–56 (3.6-7).

such as 'The fear of the LORD (*yirat Hashem*) is the beginning of wisdom' (Prov 9:10) and likewise many characters in the Bible are extolled for fearing God.[4] For example, Abraham does not reveal to Abimelech that Sarah is his wife since 'surely there is no fear of God in this place' (Gen 20:11), implying that fear of God is a virtue that is lacking in Abimelech's kingdom. Similarly, the fear of God is a positive trait in the story of Joseph who promises his brothers a fair treatment because 'I fear God' (Gen 42:18); it is also the fear of God that compelled the Egyptian midwives to refrain from following orders to kill the Israelite male children because they 'feared God, and did not as the king of Egypt commanded them' (Ex 1:17). Rabbinic literature later develops this concept, referring to it as the 'fear of heaven' (*yirat shamayim*), and treats it as the highest religious virtue. Indeed, the rabbis state that 'Everything is in the hands of Heaven except the fear of Heaven (*yirat shamayim*)' and 'Anyone who has learning [Torah] but not the fear of Heaven (*yirat shamayim*) is like a treasurer who is given the inner keys but not the outer keys. How will he enter?'[5] Hence, it seems that the wisdom of the Torah can only be fully realized through the fear of God. In fact, the rabbis suggest that one cannot entirely gain entry to the Torah's depths without possessing the appropriate awe, which in their view, is a crucial aspect of this type of fear.

Aristotle and the Bible (and later Rabbinic texts) clearly offer divergent positions on the question of fear, especially regarding the question of whether fear should be overcome through courage or whether fear is a desirable element of human striving. One of the most cogent attempts to reconcile these two seemingly contradictory approaches to fear is undertaken by the great medieval Jewish

4. Similar permutations of the statement that fear of the Lord is the beginning of wisdom can be at Prov 1:7, 8:12–13, 15:33 and Ps 111:10. For an overview of the meaning of this concept in biblical literature, see: Job Jindo, 'On the Biblical Notion of the "Fear of God" as a Condition for Human Existence', in *Biblical Interpretation* 19, no. 4–5 (2011): 433–453.
5. Babylonian Talmud Berakhot 33b and Shabbat 31b. The full plethora of rabbinic sources and interpretations regarding *yirat shamayim* have been explored in depth in Byron Sherwin, 'Fear of God', in *Contemporary Jewish Religious Thought*, edited by Arthur A Cohen and Paul Mendes-Flohr (New York: The Free Press, 1987), 245–254 and Warren Zev Harvey, '*Yirat Shamayim* in Jewish Thought', in *Yirat Shamayim: The Awe, Reverence and Fear of God*, edited by Marc D Stern (New York: Yeshiva University Press, 2008), 1–26.

philosopher, Moses Maimonides, who attempts to synthesize the Arabic-Aristotelian tradition with the Biblical-Rabbinic tradition in his *Commentary on the Mishnah*, the *Mishneh Torah*, and the *Guide of the Perplexed*. Maimonides articulates the position that the Torah advocates two distinct approaches to fear: (i) cultivating an ethics of moral and intellectual courage, overcoming fear by bravely advancing the pursuit of knowledge, and using that knowledge to improve the world, and (ii) fostering an ethics of awe, by recognizing the human limitations on comprehending the highest levels of nature, leading to acts of loving-kindness and compassion towards all.

The foundation of these two positions is laid out by Maimonides at the beginning of the *Mishneh Torah* in the *Book of Knowledge, Laws of the Foundations of the Torah* 2.2:

> And what is the way of loving Him and fearing Him? When a man reflects upon His wondrous great works and creatures and perceives from them His inestimable and infinite wisdom, he at once loves, praises, glorifies, and years greatly to know the Great Name—as David said: *My soul thirsteth for God, for the living God* [Ps 42:3]. And when he mediates on these things themselves, he at once recoils (*nirta'*) in a start, and will fear (*ve-yira'*) and tremble (*ve-yifḥad*) and know that he is a small (*qetanah*), lowly (*shfalah*), dark (*a'felah*) creature standing with slight insignificant understanding (*da'at qalah me'uṭah*) before [Him who is] perfect in understanding.[6]

Maimonides then continues to expand upon this theme at *Laws of the Foundations of the Torah* 4.12:

> When a man reflects on these things and acknowledges all the created things, from angel and sphere [to] man and the like, and sees the wisdom of the Holy one (blessed be He) in all the formed and created things, he increases the love for God. His soul thirsts, his flesh longs to love God (blessed be He). He will fear (*ve-yira'*) and tremble (*ve-yifḥad*) on account of his lowliness (*me-shifluto*), wretchedness (*ve-daluto*), and

6. Maimonides, *Mishneh Torah: The Code of Maimonides*, ed. Yohai Makbili (Israel: Or Vishua, 2009), 35 (Laws of the Foundations of the Torah, 2:2). English translation from Ralph Lerner, *Maimonides' Empire of Light: Popular Enlightenment in an Age of Belief* (Chicago: University of Chicago Press, 2000), 144.

> insignificance (*ve-kaluto*) when he compares himself to one of the great holy bodies. All the more [when he compares himself with] one of the pure forms that are separate from matter and have never at all been combined with matter. It will dawn upon him that he is like a vessel full of shame and disgrace, worthless and defective.[7]

As outlined by Maimonides, the love of God is the courageous quest to comprehend the teleological structure of nature, such that everything is purposefully ordered. Hence, the more one is aware of the *telos,* the more one feels closer to God. The fear of God, however, is the humble realization that the conclusions reached are limited and perhaps incorrect due to the physical nature of the human condition in contrast to God. The courageous quest for knowledge leads down the path to create a more just society, while the impulse to recoil in awe reached from one's limited comprehension leads to acts of love and compassion based on the shared position of human weakness. The human being needs both self-assurance and self-criticism. These two emotions are complementary.

The Psychological Origin of Fear

Maimonides follows Aristotle in presenting fear as an extreme that is situated far from the mean of the moral virtue of courage.[8] In fact, an extreme such as fear is considered by Maimonides to be a deficiency, or a symptom of a sick soul. Yet in his religious writings, Maimonides does not diagnose the specific reason why individuals fall prey to these extremes. He does however diagnose the psychological basis of fear as a mental and physical debility in his late medical work, *On The Regimen of Health.*[9] There he explains that fear originates from two sources: either the inability to escape the trauma of past loss, such as the death of a loved one or the loss of wealth; or the dread of a poten-

7. Maimonides, *Mishneh Torah*, 39 (Laws of the Foundations of the Torah, 4:12). English translation from Ralph Lerner, *Maimonides' Empire of Light*, 152.
8. Maimonides, 'Eight Chapters', in *Ethical Writings of Maimonides*, edited by Raymond L Weiss and CE Butterworth (New York: New York University Press, 1975), 67.
9. Maimonides, *On the Regimen of Health: A New Parallel Arabic-English Translation*, edited and translated by Gerrit Bos (Leiden: Brill, 2019), 108–110 (3.16).

tial misfortune that could occur to one in the future. Maimonides sees fear as originating in a false deterministic view of nature and thus, he counsels the fearful individual to oppose this type of thinking by taking the opposite approach: being hopeful for the future:

> Everything that someone anticipates belongs to the category of something possible that may happen or may not happen. And just as someone may be sad and distressed lest something he dreads might occur, in the same way one should dilate one's soul with lasting expectation and hope that perhaps the opposite of what he anticipates might occur, since both what he anticipates and its opposite are possible.[10]

Maimonides' practical lesson is that there is no benefit in living a life of distress due to being paralyzed by fear. The future is filled with multiple possibilities and it is as likely that a good and positive outcome will occur to you in the future as the negative outcome that you dread. As a result, Maimonides advocates that it is more productive in life to be hopeful and work towards one's goals, than to be paralyzed by fear of a deleterious outcome that is no more likely than the beneficial one.

Problematic Fear I: Fear of Divine Punishment

The fear of divine punishment as the motivation behind religious practice is difficult to gauge in Maimonides' writings, as at times it seems to be an approach that is endorsed by Maimonides, and at other times, condemned. In Maimonides' earlier *Book of Commandments*, he seems to look favorably upon this position, listing the fear of God as the fourth positive commandment and explaining that it is one that requires awareness of divine punishment. He writes that we should 'not be at ease and self-confident, but to expect His punishment at all times.'[11] Yet in Maimonides' later *Mishneh Torah*, he expresses a negative view of this earlier position. In the first book, the *Laws of the Foundations of the Torah*, Maimonides presents love and fear as equal, so that fear essentially means awe. However, in the final

10. Maimonides, *On the Regimen of Health*, 110.
11. Maimonides, *The Commandments (Sefer ha-Mitzvot)*, translated by Charles B Chavel (London: The Soncino Press, 1976), 5.

book, the *Laws of Repentance*, he presents love as superior to fear, since here he suggests that fear motivates people to act for the sake of reward and punishment.[12] He identifies this approach in the *Laws of Repentance* with that of those who do not know better because of ignorance; for such people, the commandments are merely a means to their own success, with the implication that one who follows them because of reward or punishment does not really care about God, but is using God to benefit oneself. However, Maimonides does admit that this form of worship has a pedagogical advantage: it trains people in the right method to worship God, even if it is for the wrong reason—that is, until they have acquired the appropriate knowledge, when they would act for the right reason.[13] He writes that

> When instructing the young, women or the illiterate generally, we teach them to serve God out of fear or for the sake of reward till their knowledge increases and they have attained a large measure of wisdom. Then we reveal to them this secret, little by little, and train them by easy stages till they have grasped and comprehended it, and serve God out of love.[14]

Indeed, utilising the fear of punishment for educational purposes is described by Maimonides as being akin to parenting: you reward and punish children for good and bad behavior with the hope that as they grow older and mature they will come to see the value of such behavior as good; they will no longer need the threat of reward and punishment and will eventually understand the reason why the action is valuable in itself. While it is not clear that everyone graduates from

12. Maimonides, *Mishneh Torah*, 35, 39 (Laws of the Foundations of the Torah, 2:2, 4:12) and 88 (Laws of Repentance 10:1–2). This contradiction has been noted in David Hartman, *Maimonides: Torah and Philosophic Quest* (Philadelphia: Jewish Publication Society, 1976), 265 n61; Howard Kreisel, *Maimonides' Political Thought: Studies in Ethics, Law and the Human Ideal* (Albany: State University of New York Press, 1999), 258–259. Cf. Joseph Kafih's comments in his edition of the *Mishneh Torah* on Maimonides, *Sefer Mishneh Torah*, ed. Joseph Kafih, volume 1, on Foundations 2:2 and Repentance 10:2 (Jerusalem: Machon Mishnat ha-Rambam, 1984), pp. and Eliyahu Nagar, 'Fear of God in Maimonides' Teaching (A Reexamination)', in *Da'at*, 39 (1997), 89–99.
13. Maimonides, *Mishneh Torah*, 85 (Laws of Repentance 10:1).
14. Maimonides, *Mishneh Torah*, 85 (Laws of Repentance 10:5). English translation with slight modifications from Maimonides, *Mishneh Torah: The Book of Knowledge*, trans. Moses Hyamson (New York: Feldheim, 1974), 93a.

this childhood stage, it is the ideal toward which to strive. Thus, the fear to which Maimonides refers as an ideal equivalent to love in the *Laws of the Foundations of the Torah*, (to be discussed further below), is not the same as the fear of punishment that ends the *Laws of Repentance* as the latter is the basic form of fear, while the former is a mode of fear that functions on a more advanced and higher level.

Problematic Fear II: Fear of Physical Death and Idolatry

Another type of fear that needs explication in Maimonides' writings is the fear of physical death in a dangerous and potentially life-threatening situation. This is the fear that prevented the Israelites from directly entering Canaan, and which, according to Maimonides, required them to wander in the desert for forty years. The prolonged period in the desert was needed in order to build up their physical courage, which would then prepare them to engage the nations of the land in war. Hence, Maimonides highlights the biblical statement 'God did not lead them by way of the land of the Philistines, although it was nearer; for God said, "The people may have a change of heart when they see war, and return to Egypt"' (Exod 13:17–18). He interprets this verse twice in the *Guide* both at III 24 and III 32, where he writes:

> And it is known that but for their misery and weariness in the desert, they would not have been able to conquer the land and to fight . . . For prosperity (*rafāhiya*) does away with courage (*al-shajā'ah*), whereas a hard life and fatigue necessarily produce courage (*al-shajā'ah*).[15]

> For just as it is not in the nature of man that, after having been brought up in slavish service occupied with clay, bricks, and similar things, he should all of a sudden wash off from his hands the dirt deriving from them and proceed immediately to fight against the *children of Anak* . . . The deity used a gracious ruse in causing them to wander perplexedly in the desert until their souls became courageous (*tashjja'tu*)—it being well know that life in the desert and lack of comforts for

15. Moses Maimonides, *The Guide of the Perplexed*, translated by Shlomo Pines (Chicago: University of Chicago Press, 1963), 500 (III 24).

> the body necessarily develop courage (*al-shajāʿah*) whereas the opposite circumstances necessarily develop cowardice (*al-jubn*)—and until, moreover, people were born who were not accustomed to humiliation and servitude . . .[16]

Maimonides offers two seemingly contradictory explanations for the fearfulness and cowardice resulting from the Israelites' enslavement in Egypt. In the first passage, he attributes it to the culture of prosperity in Egypt, implying that its prevailing ethos was one of comfort and ease, rather than toughness and hard work. In the second passage, he points to the fact that as slaves, the Israelites were compelled by their taskmasters to become meek and submissive. While the explanations at III 24 and III 32 may appear to contradict each other at first glance, presenting the Israelites as both affected by the laxity of their enslaved status as well as by the cruelty of their oppressors, his point here seems to be that as slaves the Hebrews did menial unthinking labor, such that the slave leads an easy and facile but unchallenging life in that all decisions are made by others.

The connection between the two and its outcome as physical fear can perhaps be further explained by examining the political implications of the prevailing idolatry in Egypt at the time. If one looks at how Maimonides views idolatry, it seems that he understands it as a theological representation of materialism. From this perspective, all that exists is the physical world of matter, so that the main goal of life is to increase one's worldly gain.[17] Happiness is therefore found in the amount of worldly goods obtained such as money, food, pleasure, honor, etc. The problem with such a worldview is that physical desires are unlimited and insatiable. The more one has, the more one desires, such that one is never satisfied with what one has.[18] This human weakness leads shrewd manipulators to create false religions and 'idols' for the weak-minded whose 'gods' falsely promise to fulfill all their physical desires. These false prophets then oppress and control the masses for their own personal gain. As Maimonides writes, 'These practices are all false and deceptive, and employed by the ancient idolaters to

16. Maimonides, *Guide*, 528 (III 32).
17. Leo Strauss notes this in describing 'corporealism as the hidden premise of idolatry' (Leo Strauss, 'How to Begin to Study *The Guide of the Perplexed*', in *Guide*, xlii).
18. Maimonides, *Guide*, 445 (III 12).

deceive the peoples of various countries and to derive benefit from them (*kedei she-yinnahu 'aḥareihem*)'.[19] Egypt is an example of such a culture, whose material prosperity depended on the enslavement of others, and where the majority of people are weak and afraid, other than those in the upper echelons of society. Maimonides describes this type of exploitation in his discussion of the phrase 'excruciating labor' (*farekh*), the term used to denote the tormenting work that the Egyptians imposed on the Israelites (Exod 1:13). In the *Laws of Slavery*, he interprets this to mean labor that has no limit and is essentially unnecessary, as it imposes useless tasks onto people to turn them into tools so as to control them.[20]

According to Maimonides, the only way for the Israelites to overcome this fear of physical death and develop courage against life threatening obstacles is to learn how to live in the harsh conditions of the desert. In both Maimonides' and Al-Farabi's thought, the desert represents a setting with the least amount of physical comfort, one which would naturally create courageous habits due to its difficult environment.[21] As the leader of the Israelites, Moses needed to transform a nation of slaves into a nation with a strong military will that could conquer a land and build a state. His knowledge of both God and nature gave him the ability to trick the Israelites into wandering in the desert for forty years, for the purpose of creating a state of misery and lack of comfort which, combined with freedom, was essential for training them to be courageous in battle.[22] This means overcoming the fear of physical death since this must be achieved

19. Maimonides, *Mishneh Torah*, 76 (Laws of Idolatry 11:16). English translation with slight modifications from *Mishneh Torah* (Hyamson), 80a.
20. Maimonides, *Mishneh Torah*, 1083 (Laws of Slaves 1:6).
21. Abu-Nasr Al-Farabi, 'Selected Aphorisms of a Statesman', in *Alfarabi, The Political Writings: Selected Aphorisms and Other Texts*, translated by Charles E Butterworth (Ithaca: Cornell University Press, 2001), 22 (No 23) and Maimonides, *Mishneh Torah*, 52 (Laws of Character Traits 6:1). Maimonides conceives of the desert in this way also in the 'Letter to Yemen', where he counsels those who cannot get away by emigration from an evil regime which persecutes Jews, also to escape to the desert. See Maimonides, 'Letter to Yemen', in *Maimonides Reader*, edited by Isadore Twersky (Springfield: Library of Jewish Studies, 1972), 448.
22. Maimonides, *Guide*, 500 (3.24) and 528 (3.32). See Shlomo Pines, 'Ibn Khaldun and Maimonides: A Comparison between Two Texts', in *Studia Islamica*, 32 (1970), 170. Maimonides appears to elaborate and develop much farther this idea proposed by Abraham Ibn Ezra on Exod 3:17.

before entering the land of Israel where the Israelites will encounter war and risk their lives in battle to defend themselves against potential enemies.

Solution I: Fear as Incrementalism

Fear also plays a vital role in the way in which prophecy is attained as a necessary restraint on moving too quickly to obtain the proper prophetic knowledge, thus leading to failure. Maimonides considers Moses to be unique and incomparable to both earlier and later biblical prophets, listing four differences between Moses' prophecy and that of other prophets.[23] The third difference to which he makes reference is that all other prophets experienced fear when receiving prophecy, such that they were 'filled with fear (*yere'in*), consternation (*ve-nivhalin*) and became physically weak (*u-mitmogegin*).' He contrasts this with Moses whose prophecy he says was without terror and dread, as if he were speaking to a friend.[24] The common fear among other prophets reflects the influence of the imagination, while the lack of fear in Moses' prophecy refers to the rational character of his prophecy without influence of the imagination, 'because of the strength of his union with the [Agent] intelligence'[25] This differs from the fear that Moses experiences after hearing God's message at the burning bush, where it says 'And Moses hid his face, for he was afraid (*yare*) to look at God' (Exod 3:6). As Maimonides clarifies in *Guide* I 5, the fear described at the burning bush is a reflection of Moses' patience and moderation in taking the incremental steps to master

23. Maimonides, *Commentary on the Mishna*, volume iv, 212–214; *Mishneh Torah*, 42 (Laws of the Foundations of the Torah, 7:6); and *Guide*, 367–368 (II 35) and 378–380 (II 39).
24. Maimonides, *Mishneh Torah*, 42 (Laws of the Foundations of the Torah, 7:6). English translation in Maimonides, *Mishneh Torah* (Hyamson), 43a. For an earlier version of this statement, see *Mishnah, 'Im Perush Mosheh ben Maimon* [*Commentary on the Mishna*] (Jerusalem: Mossad ha-Rav Kook, 1963–1967), volume iv, 214.
25. Maimonides, *Commentary on the Mishna*, volume iv, 214. English translation of Menachem Kellner in Kellner, *Dogma in Medieval Jewish Thought: From Maimonides to Abravanel* (Oxford: Littman Library of Jewish Civilization, 2004), 14.

the prerequisites before attempting to apprehend God.[26] According to this definition of fear,

> He should not make categoric affirmations in favor of the first opinion that occurs to him, and should not, from the outset, strain and impel his thoughts toward the apprehension of the deity; he should rather feel awe (*yastaḥiyyu*) and hold back until he gradually elevates himself.

Moses is afraid of moving too quickly and thus not taking the right steps to achieve the results. This is similar to the kind of incremental learning recommended by Maimonides in the Dedicatory Letter of the *Guide*, where he says that the proper order of study for his pupil Joseph is to first master the basic sciences before approaching the weightier topic of metaphysics, or discerning the science of God. As he makes clear in the *Guide*, Maimonides is concerned that if a student longs for the answers too much then he will move too quickly and not follow the right order and method to achieve his goal.[27]

In the same vein, Maimonides posits that Moses' fearful encounter with God through the burning bush at Exodus 3 represents the beginning of his philosophic quest to know God, one that is cautious and methodical. He traces the evolution of this quest back to when an angel appeared to Moses in Exodus 3:2, 'And the angel of the Lord appeared to him' with the angel, in this context, referring to a prophetic vision through the imaginative faculty.[28] For Maimonides, a vision can be explained as a manifestation of the imaginative faculty reaching its highest perfection. As he puts it: a vision 'signifies that the imaginative faculty achieves so great a perfection of action that it sees the thing as if it were outside, and that the thing whose origin is due to it appears to have come to it by the way of external sensation.'[29] As such, the image of the burning bush is a creation in Moses' imagination derived from the Active Intellect, but one that leads him to knowledge of God. Through his gradual training, he progresses with

26. Warren Zev Harvey, 'Maimonides on Human Perfection, Awe and Politics', in *The Thought of Moses Maimonides*, edited Ira Robinson, Lawrence Kaplan, and Julien Bauer (Lewiston, NY: Edwin Mellen, 1990), 6.
27. Maimonides, *Guide*, 3–4 (Dedicatory Letter).
28. Maimonides, *Guide*, 264–265 (II 6) and 576 (III 45).
29. Maimonides, *Guide*, 370 (II 36).

the proper fear as incrementalism from his initial prophecy through the imaginative faculty to his later perfectly rational prophecy whereby he 'speaks mouth to mouth' with God and 'beholds the likeness of the Lord' (Numb 12:8).[30]

Maimonides also interprets the sacrificial service in the Torah as reflecting the same type of incrementalism. According to Maimonides, Moses knew not to radically tear the Israelites away from the pagan worship to which they were accustomed in Egypt; hence he did not introduce them too quickly to the intellectual worship of God. Instead, Moses modified their existing practices so that over time they would come closer to proper worship.[31] Here he also interprets the citation, discussed above, that 'God did not lead them by way of the land of the Philistines' (Exod 13:17–18) as a metaphor for Moses' incrementalism in structuring the Torah in such as way so as to gradually teach the Israelites to acquire the proper courage needed for knowing God.[32]

Solution II: Moral and Political Courage

Maimonides states that a key quality of prophecy is overcoming the fear to speak out and act in the public sphere with the moral and political courage to challenge the conventional opinions held by political authorities, often telling them directly that they are in the wrong. According to Maimonides, this type of courage is rooted in the natural force of spiritedness or boldness (*iqdām*), especially prevalent in prophets. Indeed, he compares this instinctive spiritedness or boldness to the natural impulse of repulsion or self-defense.[33] He notes that in its raw form, it can be manifested in extremes of fear or rashness as he illustrates by the analogy of how different people respond to confronting an animal: 'you may find among people some

30. Alvin J Reines, 'Maimonides' Concept of Mosaic Prophecy,' in *Hebrew Union College Annual*, 40/41 (1969–1970), 336 and Howard Kreisel, *Judaism as Philosophy: Studies in Maimonides and the Medieval Jewish Philosophers of Provence* (Brighton: Academic Studies Press, 2015), 324–325.
31. Maimonides, *Guide*, 525–531 (III 32).
32. Maimonides, *Guide*, 527–528 (III 32).
33. Maimonides, *Guide*, 376–378 (II 38). See: Raymond Weiss, *Maimonides' Ethics: The Encounter of Philosophic and Religious Morality* (Chicago: University of Chicago Press, 1991), 163–164.

who will advance upon a lion, while others flee from a mouse.' In Maimonides' view, the channeling of the natural force of spiritedness or boldness to overcome fear properly arises as a result of the perfection of the intellect, such that 'when the intellect overflows toward them, these two faculties become very greatly strengthened.' Moreover, the prophet has the reasoning power of divination, which is a rational process of quick thinking about when, where and on whom to act regarding 'warnings concerning great future events.' The certainty the prophet possesses in his message along with his rhetorical ability to convince the audience through the imaginative faculty, gives him the strength to overcome his fear and courageously confront a powerful leader with his vital message.

The biblical way of expressing this phenomenon of overcoming fear in the moral and political realm is for Maimonides the expression the 'spirit of God' (*ruaḥ elohim*), referring to the first and second degrees of prophecy in *Guide* II 45. One apparent difficulty with associating *ruaḥ elohim* with courage is that Maimonides makes no explicit mention of *iqdām* in that chapter. However, as noted by Abrabanel in his *Commentary on the Guide*, Maimonides hints that these first two grades of prophecy are in fact forms of courage; this can be seen in his use of similar language that directly alludes to other references he makes to virtue, even though he does not specifically mention *iqdām*.[34] But while both are rooted in spiritedness, in II 38 Maimonides appears to be talking about the natural impulse that controls courage, while in II 45 it is the same impulse controlled by reason and channeled toward a noble purpose, thus truly making it a virtue. These two lower degrees of prophecy, in which the actor has *ruaḥ elohim* attributed to his actions, represent two modes of moral courage: courage to act for the truth in society (first degree) and courage to speak the truth in society (second degree). The first type of courage is exemplified in the actions of biblical judges and kings and the second type of courage is exemplified in the authorship of biblical wisdom literature.[35] It is this supreme moral and political courage of the prophet, both in words and deeds, which Maimonides suggests

34. Alvin Reines, *Maimonides and Abrabanel on Prophecy* (Cincinnati: Hebrew Union College Press, 1970), 186–187. My interpretation draws upon Abrabanel's connection between Guide II 38 and II 45, though does not take his argument fully in the direction he does.

35. Maimonides, *Guide*, 396–398 (II 45).

is needed to uphold truth in society and to check the interest of the king and other powerful leaders of that society. Thus, the prophets do not fear the king, the royal authorities, or the masses, since they are motivated by the 'spirit of God,' which is the faculty of courage. The spirit of God is an alternative to fear, enabling one to overcome fear.

Solution III: Fear as Awe

According to Maimonides, fear becomes infused with awe when man becomes aware of the limitations of human knowledge and the fundamentally weak physical condition of humanity. In fact, Maimonides views this as an essential lesson of the story of the binding of Isaac (Genesis 22). The story ends with the words of the angel stating, 'for now I know that you fear (*yere*) God, since you have not withheld your son, your favored one, from me' (Gen 22:12). In fact, Maimonides regards this story as 'the highest of the degrees of the prophets . . . after the perfection of the rational faculties' while simultaneously demonstrating the limits of love and fear of God, 'up to what limit they must reach.'[36] Maimonides suggests that this story not only has a deep philosophic meaning but also that it occurred in a prophetic vision, thus making it a parable whose meaning must be pondered and discerned.[37] In other words, the events concerning the binding of Isaac, according to this interpretation, were not historical, but took place in a prophetic vision.

Furthermore, Maimonides seems to intentionally link the story of the binding of Isaac at Genesis 22 with the story of the Garden of Eden at Genesis 2–3 through the character of Samael, the wicked angel that is equivalent to the character Satan, who confronts both Eve (through the Serpent) and Abraham in various midrashim.[38] Thus, Maimonides appears to be suggesting that one should inter-

36. Maimonides, *Guide*, 402 (II 45) and 500 (III 24).
37. Maimonides, *Guide*, 386 (II 41) and 501–502 (III 24). See: Abraham Nuriel, 'Maimonides on parables not explicitly identified as such,' in *Da'at* 25 (1990): 88–89.
38. Maimonides, *Guide*, 356 (II 30). Samael appears in *Genesis Rabbah* 56.4 with regards to the binding of Isaac and *Pirqe de-Rabbi Eliezer* 13 with regards to the Garden of Eden. For an overview of Maimonides' intertextual citations in *Guide* III 24, see: James Diamond, *Maimonides and the Hermeneutics of Concealment* (Albany: State University of New York Press, 2002), 131–150.

pret the story of the binding of Isaac allegorically in the same way he interpreted the tale of the Garden of Eden in *Guide* I 2. If, in the Garden of Eden, Adam, Eve and the Serpent represent form, matter and the imagination, then one can similarly read Abraham, Isaac and the midrashic addition of Samael to respectively represent form, matter and the imagination.[39] As such, the two stories impart a similar message, but in different ways: the Garden of Eden represents the impossibility of being a pure intellect without the imagination and physical desires, while the binding of Isaac represents the attempt of the human intellect to transcend the body and the imagination, but reaches the conclusion that this is not possible or desirable. Hence, God's command for Abraham to sacrifice Isaac to Him can be interpreted as the allegorical expression of Abraham's attempt to intellectually know God such that he would liberate himself from his corporeal existence (metaphorically 'kill') in order to focus on pure intellectual conjunction.

Moreover, the way that the story ends—with Abraham not killing Isaac, followed by the message about the fear of God—is highly significant for Maimonides. According to his reading, when the angel stopped Abraham from killing Isaac, this is a metaphor for Abraham reaching a specific level of knowledge: the realization that he cannot have apodictic demonstrative knowledge of God and thus must live and act through his corporeal existence, symbolized by his son Isaac. Furthermore, the fear of God that the angel reveals to Abraham is his recognition of intellectual humility. Maimonides makes this very point about the fear of God following from the intellectual knowledge and love of God in *Guide* III 52:

> Know that when perfect men understand this, they achieve such humility, such awe and fear of God, such reverence and shame before Him, may He be exalted—and this in ways that pertain to true reality, not to imagination—that their secret conduct with their wives and in latrines is like their public conduct with other people.[40]

39. Maimonides, *Guide*, 24–26 (I 2). The nature of Satan is explored further at *Guide*, 488–490 (III 22). See: Warren Zev Harvey, 'Three Theories of the Imagination in 12th Century Jewish Philosophy', in *Intellect and Imagination in Medieval Philosophy*, volume 1, edited by Maria Candida Pacheco and Jose F Meirinhos (Turnhout: Brepols, 2006), 300–301.
40. Maimonides, *Guide*, 629 (III 52).

The humility that arises from the fear of God is the recognition of a common human fragility and smallness in the larger expanse of existence. For Maimonides, this inspires the great rabbis to act with humility and modesty, as is evident in the Talmudic examples he cites, such as, 'It is prohibited for a person to walk even four cubits with an upright posture' implying arrogance.[41] In fact, Abraham's discovery of humility and awe through the Akedah story leads him to become the exemplar of kindness and compassion for all people. Maimonides writes that the descendants of Abraham are merciful to all, that charity is an identifying mark among them, and that Abraham instituted the ways of loving-kindness by selflessly welcoming guests to his home.[42] Although Abraham came to the rational knowledge of God, which enabled him to teach others and help them increase their wisdom, he also realized the limitations of metaphysical knowledge. This led him to the conclusion that human beings are also weak and fragile creatures requiring mercy and compassion in order to improve their human condition.

Conclusion

Bonhoeffer's sermon, 'Overcoming Fear', not only echoes Maimonides' analysis of the multiple sources of human fear but it also emphasises the religious calling to triumph over fear which both thinkers derive from the Bible. As we have seen, Maimonides incorporates multiple definitions and types of fear in his writings, some positive and others negative. Drawing on his reading of biblical stories, he shows that living with fear of divine punishment by an authoritarian God or living in fear of physical death in an oppressive idolatrous culture are both forms of weakness that attempt to minimize human initiative and striving. Instead of submitting to fear, Maimonides advocates for both an ideal of courage and an ideal of awe. The proper knowledge of God must be acquired by avoiding the extremes of fear and rashness, not advancing too quickly, but with the courage to know more. This leads to morally and politically courageous actions to fight against injustices and improve society. However, the limitations of how much knowledge can be achieved with certainty leads to awe. It incorporates the recognition that human beings are generally weak, and this

41. BT Kiddushin 31a.
42. Maimonides, *Mishneh Torah*, 1092 (Laws of Slaves 9:8), 562 (Laws of Gifts to the Poor 10.1), and 1232 (Laws of Mourning 14:2)

knowledge serves as a stimulus for people to act with compassion towards each other. As a result, one may say that Maimonides' unique integration of Aristotelian and biblical ideas points to how to achieve a proper balance of courage and awe, by bringing out the best of both, thereby showing how it might be possible to live a life that is both heroic and humble.

Vol 7 No 1&2/2019

Can Evolution Make Sense of Fear? Lessons from Bonhoeffer and Darwin

Joseph Bulbulia and Dominic DP Johnson[1]

> In thoughts from the visions of the night, when deep sleep falleth on men, fear came upon me, and trembling, which made all my bones to shake. Then a spirit passed before my face; the hair of my flesh stood up. It stood still, but I could not discern the form thereof: an image was before my eyes, there was silence, and I heard a voice, saying, Shall mortal man be more just than God? Shall a man be more pure than his Maker? (The book of Job 4:13).
>
> —quoted by Charles Darwin in *The Expression of the Emotions in Man and Animals*[2]

Introduction

In the dark days of 1933 Germany, Dietrich Bonhoeffer delivered his famous sermon on 'overcoming fear' at a vespers service in Berlin. Using lessons from the Bible, he pointed out that fear can be an immensely destructive force, undermining courage and confidence, making people shy away from facing up to (or facing down) impending dangers, and allowing evil forces to rise to the ascendency—in his case with devastating results for Europe and the world.

Bonhoeffer's remarkable sermon deserves its praise, and remains a striking motivational piece for our own times of social and political challenges. Yet how reasonable is it to expect that fear can, with words, be tamed? Or, at least, how easy or hard is it to do? More generally,

---

1. Authors arranged alphabetically.
2. Charles Darwin, *The Expression of the Emotions in Man and Animals* (1872), 291.

by what pathways might people be directed to overcome their fears? Bonhoeffer was surely right about the moral failures of Germany in the 1930s. Here we apply an evolutionary lens to fear to investigate whether Bonhoeffer's sermon might be more effectively channelled to combat fear's destructive political embodiments.

Our argument will be as follows: Humans are far from calculating, rational actors that weigh up and respond to events in an even-handed way. Instead, we rely on a myriad of evolved physiological and psychological dispositions that help us to make the many complex judgments, decisions, actions and interactions with others needed to survive and thrive in life. Across the animal kingdom, *emotional states* in particular evolved as a powerful way to regulate organisms' behaviours. Yet, emotional states present something of an enigma to biology. As Darwin observed, it is puzzling that the *inward* motivational states of emotions are accompanied by *outward* emotional expressions. Such a puzzle is particularly acute in the case of fear. Why would an animal under threat project fear to its audience, including its menace? Here, we draw on Bonhoeffer's reflections about the debilitating effects of fear in 1930s Germany, to consider how evolutionary principles shed new light on some long-standing questions about the role of fear in social and political organisation. These insights are important because they reveal an unexpected role for how fear—in the right contexts—may have been (and can still be) channelled to produce social benefit, rather than social ruin.

Darwin's Evolutionary Puzzle of Emotions

Why did fear evolve? From an evolutionary standpoint, that organisms feel strong aversion is hardly surprising. Fear prompts an organism to avoid biological hazards—perhaps the single most important imperative for the survival and persistence of any animal.[3] However, fear is more than aversion. Like other strong emotional states fear is typically accompanied by dramatic emotional expressions. With fear, one discloses one's motivational cards in a high-stakes poker game of life. Among his numerous astute observations, Charles Darwin considered three perplexing facets of strong emotions such as fear.

3. DT Blumstein, *The Nature of Fear: Survival Lessons from the Wild* (Cambridge, MA: Harvard University Press, 2020).

Figure 1[4] Image in Darwin's *The Expression of the Emotions in Man and Animals*, from Duchenne's experiments revealing the contraction of the platysma muscle as 'the muscle of fright'.[5]

First, strong emotions typically produce *involuntary* physical responses:

> . . . certain actions which we recognize as expressive of certain states of the mind, are the direct result of the constitution of the nervous system . . . Of course every movement which we make is determined by the constitution of the nervous system; but actions performed in obedience to the will, or through habit, or through the principle of antithesis, are here as far as possible excluded. Our present subject is very obscure, but, from its importance, must be discussed at some little length; and it is always advisable to perceive clearly our ignorance . . . [consider] . . . trembling of the muscles, which is common to man and to many, or most, of the lower animals. Trembling is of no service, often of much disservice, and cannot have been at first acquired through the will, and then rendered habitual in association with any emotion. Trembling is excited in different individuals in very different degrees, and by the most diversified causes—by cold to the surface, before fever-fits, although the temperature of the body is then above the

4. Image source: https://commons.wikimedia.org/wiki/File:Terror,_from_Darwin%27s_Expression_of_Emotions_in_Man . . .._Wellcome_L0049512.jpg
5. Darwin, *The Expression of the Emotions in Man and Animals*, 299.

> normal standard; in blood-poisoning, delirium tremens, and other diseases; by general failure of power in old age; by exhaustion after excessive fatigue . . . Of all emotions, fear notoriously is the most apt to induce trembling.[6]

Darwin noticed that on the face of it (so to speak) such automated expressions are 'are of no service, often of much disservice, and cannot have been acquired by the will'.[7]

The second perplexing feature of emotional expressions that Darwin noticed is that these automated responses are *readily interpreted by observers as indicators of inward motivation.* Darwin reports the following description from an informant:

> Mr Bell [. . .] described [. . .] an agony of terror and of despair, which he witnessed in a murderer, whilst carried to the place of execution in Turin. On each side of the car the officiating priests were seated; and in the centre sat the criminal himself. It was impossible to witness the condition of this unhappy wretch without terror; and yet, as if impelled by some strange infatuation, it was equally impossible not to gaze upon an object so wild, so full of horror. He seemed about thirty-five years of age; of large and muscular form; his countenance marked by strong and savage features; half naked, pale as death, agonized with terror, every limb strained in anguish, his hands clenched convulsively, the sweat breaking out on his bent and contracted brow, he kissed incessantly the figure of our Saviour, painted on the flag which was suspended before him; but with an agony of wildness and despair, of which nothing ever exhibited on the stage can give the slightest conception.[8]

What Darwin called 'the instinctive recognition of expression'[9] is perplexing because, in humans, so much communication relies on culturally acquired languages.

> . . . from the earliest days and throughout life quite beyond our control; for instance, the relaxation of the arteries of the skin

6. Darwin, *The Expression of the Emotions in Man and Animals*, 66–67.
7. Darwin, *The Expression of the Emotions in Man and Animals*, 66–67.
8. Darwin, *The Expression of the Emotions in Man and Animals*, 293.
9. Darwin, *The Expression of the Emotions in Man and Animals*, 347.

> in blushing, and the increased action of the heart in anger. We may see children, only two or three years old, and even those born blind, blushing from shame; and the naked scalp of a very young infant reddens from passion. Infants scream from pain directly after birth, and all their features then assume the same form as during subsequent years. These facts alone suffice to show that many of our most important expressions have not been learnt.[10]

The third perplexing feature of emotional expressions that Darwin noticed—which is related to the first and second puzzling features, of automation and interpretability—is that emotional expressions are *culturally ubiquitous*:

> I have endeavoured to show in considerable detail that all the chief expressions exhibited by man are the same throughout the world. This fact is interesting, as it affords a new argument in favour of the several races being descended from a single parent-stock, which must have been almost completely human in structure, and to a large extent in mind, before the period at which the races diverged from each other.[11]

We can condense these three perplexing features of emotional expression into a single riddle: how might emotional expressions have evolved to benefit organisms through involuntary, reflexive circuits that by-passes willful effort when such expressions—'are of no service, often of much disservice' to the strongly emoting organism? For example, what biological function could be served by shuddering in the face of some manifest threat?

Darwin closed *The Emotional Expressions* as follows:

> We have also seen that expression in itself, or the language of the emotions, as it has sometimes been called, is certainly of importance for the welfare of mankind. To understand, as far as possible, the source or origin of the various expressions which may be hourly seen on the faces of the men around us, not to mention our domesticated animals, ought to possess much interest for us. From these several causes, we may conclude that the philosophy of our subject has well deserved

10. Darwin, *The Expression of the Emotions in Man and Animals*, 352–353.
11. Darwin, *The Expression of the Emotions in Man and Animals*, 359.

> the attention which it has already received from several excellent observers, and that it deserves still further attention, especially from any able physiologist.[12]

Darwin recognised the importance of a biological account of emotion 'for the welfare of mankind' but did not directly speculate about functions. One of Darwin's major achievements, however, was to show that emotions are not merely internal psychological states. They are an evolved system for social communication. But to what end?

The Evolutionary Logic of Cooperation and Punishment

An evolutionary approach to fear must clarify how its automated, manifest, and culturally ubiquitous properties communicate in ways different to language. This task requires understanding that communication evolved—at least in large part—for the purposes of coordination and cooperation. As we shall see, the challenges of aligning our behaviour with others raise evolutionary problems for which automated expressions afford some remarkable solutions.

Consider, for example, the quintessential problem of ensuring cooperative interactions: how can we be sure others will be loyal and return our own efforts or favours, especially in hard times? This is difficult enough in one-on-one interactions (witness the prisoner's dilemma and the many other forms of cooperation problems in everyday social life). These problems, which are tricky even at the scale of familiar neighbours, became magnified as soon as human groups expanded from the small-scale kin groups of our evolutionary past to larger, settled groups of anonymous strangers. Studies of collective action have long found that, left unchecked, cooperation among self-interested agents dwindles over time.[13] There are just too many incentives to free-ride and too much uncertainty about if or how much others will pull their weight, especially when the stakes are high and people must take risks to help others. In an environment

12. Darwin, *The Expression of the Emotions in Man and Animals*, 366.
13. E Fehr and S Gächter, 'Altruistic punishment in humans', in *Nature*, 415 (2002): 137–140; *The Handbook of Experimental Economics*, edited by JH Kagel and AE Roth (Princeton: Princeton University Press, 1995) and M Olson, *The Logic of Collective Action: Public Goods and the Theory of Groups* (Cambridge: Harvard University Press, 1965).

in which cooperation is hard to achieve, what special conditions are available to enable cooperation to stablise and endure?[14] Notice that in a cooperation dilemma, conventional language will not necessarily resolve it. 'Trust me', 'The check is in the mail', 'My word is my bond', and similar locutions are not always effective predictors of behaviour. We seek actual bonds.

Generally, cooperation can be induced and sustained only via some other factor, but that 'some other factor' typically has to be added in order to avert the otherwise relentless undermining or failure of cooperation. One simple but powerful factor is *punishment*, and the opportunity to establish rules that render punishment predictable and reliable.[15] If people are (and anticipate) being punished for flouting the rules when everyone else is towing the line, then the price of non-cooperation can be raised above the costs of cooperation. Cheating or shirking becomes costly in itself and, thereby, cooperation can be attained. (Of course, if it is possible to *avoid* punishment, then one can potentially still reap the spoils of everyone else cooperating without contributing anything oneself, but the point is that this becomes harder and rarer wherever punishment is possible).

Solving the cooperation problem was especially important because humans didn't choose to live in groups of strangers. Rather, humans are *obligate cooperators*. Biologist Richard Alexander noted that the best evidence for human obligate cooperation comes from war. He points out that across the animal kingdom, forming into groups is a common adaptation to defend against predation.[16] Alexander argues that exactly the same problem faced humans as well; however, the difference is that human predators were not merely sabre-toothed tigers and packs of hyenas—they were mainly groups of *other humans*. Within-group cooperation thus became essential for effective intergroup competition and defense. Members of early human groups would have been highly dependent on each other for collective sur-

14. E Ostrom, *Governing the Commons: The Evolution of Institutions for Collective Action* (Cambridge University Press, 1990).
15. E Ostrom, J Walker and R Gardner 'Covenants With and Without a Sword: Self-Governance is Possible', in *The American Political Science Review*, 86/2 (1992): 404–417. https://doi.org/10.2307/1964229.
16. R Alexander, *The Biology of Moral Systems* (Berlin: De Grutyer, 1987).

vival.[17] Empirical analyses of 186 historical societies around the globe bear out Alexander's hypothesis: societies with a higher incidence of inter-group warfare tended to grow to larger group sizes, and were more likely to have moralizing codes of practice that promote in-group cooperation.[18]

In-group cooperation, and banding together against out-groups, appears to have been a fundamental tool of survival. And, perhaps most notably, *religions*—with their panoply of norm-inducing beliefs and practices—appear to have provided an important and recurrent means of achieving it. It is religious ideas and religious rituals that often appear to provide the strongest social glue binding groups together in common purpose and actions.[19] Whatever else it does, religion functions to bind people together. But why is it so effective a method?

Religion as a 'Complex Adaptive System' Promoting Cooperative Regulation and Prediction

Beginning in the 1990s, economists[20] and behavioral ecologists[21] theorised that religious systems evolved as *human communication systems* that function as a co-ordinated cooperative exchange through 'costly' behaviours. The core of the idea is that religious behaviour evolved (or was co-opted) to *authenticate* cooperative acts and responses

17. A Gat, *War in Human Civilization* (Oxford: Oxford University Press, 2006); LH Keeley, *War Before Civilization: The Myth of the Peaceful Savage* (Oxford: Oxford University Press, 1996) and RW Wrangham and L Glowacki 'Intergroup Aggression in Chimpanzees and War in Nomadic Hunter-Gatherers: Evaluating the Chimpanzee Model', in *Human Nature,* 23 (2012): 5–29.
18. FL Roes and M Raymond, 'Belief in Moralizing Gods', in *Evolution and Human Behavior: Official Journal of the Human Behavior and Evolution Society*, 24/2 (2003): 126–135.
19. R Uro, 'Ritual and Christian Origins,' in D Neufeld and R DeMaris, editors, *Understanding the Social World of the New* Testament (London: Routledge 2010): 223–235.
20. LR Iannaccone, 'Why Strict Churches Are Strong', in *The American Journal of Sociology*, 99/5 (1994): 1180–1211.
21. W Irons, 'Morality, Religion, and Evolution', in *Religion and science: History, Method, and Dialogue,* edited by WWWM Richardson (Milton Park, UK: Routledge, 1996), 375–399.

among exchange partners[22]—a way of guaranteeing loyalty and the future return of favours with costly and 'hard to fake' signals of commitment. Of course, religion cannot be reduced to a single thing, and indeed modern evolutionary approaches explicitly recognize it as a 'complex adaptive system' (defined as 'a set of interacting or interdependent elements that form an integrated whole', such that a change in one element has multiple knock-on effects on the wider system; it is 'adaptive' because the system adjusts to prevailing conditions).[23] Richard Sosis refers to religious systems as 'an exquisite, complex adaptation that serves to support extensive human cooperation and coordination, and social life as we know it'.[24]

Thus, while religions themselves represent complex *cultural* systems,[25] (one of) the effects of these cultural systems is to tap into the *biological* strata of the individual human beings that participate within them. Complex cultural ideas, practices, and beliefs are perceived, experienced by, and ultimately change the behaviour of adherents, and thus influence and are influenced by their biology. Examples of this cultural reach into our biological mechanisms range from endocrine responses to ritual participation to neurological changes in religious contemplation.[26] However sophisticated and

22. W Irons, 'Religion as Hard-to-Fake Sign of Commitment', in *Evolution and the Capacity for Commitment*, edited by R Nesse (New York: Russell Sage Foundation, 2001), 292–309 and Richard Sosis, 'Religion and Intragroup Cooperation: Preliminary Results of a Comparative Analysis of Utopian Communities', in *Cross-Cultural Research: Official Journal of the Society for Cross-Cultural Research / Sponsored by the Human Relations Area Files, Inc*, 34/1 (200): 70–87. https://doi.org/10.1177/106939710003400105
23. R Sosis, 'The Building Blocks of Religious Systems: Approaching Religion as a Complex Adaptive System', in *Evolution, Development & Complexity: Multiscale Models of Complex Adaptive Systems*, edited by JMSGY Georgiev, CL Flores Martinez, and M Price (New York: Springer, 2019), 423.
24. Sosis, 'The Building Blocks of Religious Systems', 422.
25. C Alcorta and R Sosis, 'Ritual, Emotion, and Sacred Symbols: The Evolution of Religion as An Adaptive Complex', in *Human Nature*, 16ME /4 (2005), 323–359 and ME McCullough, P Swartwout, JH Shaver, EC Carter and R Sosis (2016). 'Christian Religious Badges Instill Trust in Christian and Non-Christian Perceivers', in *Psychology of Religion and Spirituality*, 8/2 (2016): 149. https://doi.org/10.1037/rel0000045
26. P McNamara, *Where God and Science Meet: How Brain and Evolutionary Studies Alter Our Understanding of Religion* (three volumes). (Westport, CT: Praeger Perspectives, 2006) and U Schjoedt, 'The Religious Brain: A General Introduction to The Experimental Neuroscience of Religion', in *Method and Theory in the Study of Religion*, 21 (2009): 310–339.

'social' a phenomenon religion may be, its effects are made on biological organisms, and it is biological organisms that exhibit them. Signalling theorists note that religious behaviours possess the following properties:

1. Religious behaviours are "hard-to-fake" (for example, a non-believer cannot readily send credible signals of belief to those in the know).
2. Religious behaviours are markers of specific group loyalties (e.g., observing a Muslim *hafiz* recite the Koran reveals a commitment to Islam, not Roman Catholicism).
3. The groups to which religious persons belong are moral communities in which explicit norms guide behaviour (for example, in understanding someone's commitment to a religion we understand, among other things, their commitment to a moral system).

Signaling theories of religion have become widely supported (both theoretically and empirically), and the signals and their responses appear to be central to the effectiveness of religion in numerous aspects of promoting social coordination, cooperation, and organisation.[27]

However, we might press the functional question deeper. Why should *religious* communities be more effective moral communities than other cultural or linguistic groupings? Behavioural ecologists assume that psychological and physiological processes underpin

27. D Chen, 'The Economics Of Teacher Supply In Indonesia', in *Policy Research Working Papers*, 2009. https://doi.org/10.1596/1813-9450-4975; CD Lynn, JJ Paris, CA Frye and LM Schell (2015). 'Religious-Commitment Signaling and Impression Management Amongst Pentecostals: Relationships to Salivary Cortisol and Alpha-Amylase', in *Journal of Cognition and Culture*, 15/3-4 (2015): 299–319. https://doi.org/10.1163/15685373-12342152, McCullough, 'Christian Religious Badges Instill Trust in Christian and Non-Christian Perceivers'; R Soler, 'Costly Signaling, Ritual and Cooperation: Findings from Candomblé, an Afro-Brazilian Religion', Unpublished Manuscript; R Sosis, H Kress and J Boster, 'Scars for War: Evaluating Signaling Explanations for Cross-cultural Variance in Ritual Costs', in *Evolution and Human Behavior: Official Journal of the Human Behavior and Evolution Society*, 28R (2007): 234–247 and R Sosis and C Alcorta, C. (2003). 'Signaling, Solidarity, and the Sacred: The Evolution of Religious Behavior', in *Evolutionary Anthropology*, 12/6 (2003): 264–274. https://doi.org/10.1002/evan.10120

behaviour, but they are 'largely agnostic with regard to the mechanisms, both psychological and physiological, that produce adaptive responses'.[28] Instead, behavioural ecologists reverse engineer behaviour using the tools of optimality modelling. By describing the optimal use of resources, energy expenditure, foraging, sheltering, mating, parenting, helping, and so on, behavioural ecologists are able to explain otherwise baffling qualities of behaviour as adaptations to address core biological problems (often, the benefits are indirect, delayed in time, or accrue to genetic relatives). Though religious practices can look manifestly wasteful in their heavy commitment of time or resources, or as Irons puts it, 'crazy',[29] the argument is that religious behaviours evolved to signal group commitment. If so, increasing the cost of such practices can merely be the price of sending a stronger signal (although, of course, there will be some optimal level, beyond which exorbitant costs will drive group members away instead of offering incentives to remain)[30]

That's the general argument, but what about the detail? We might want to understand why, for example, recurring features of religions propagate, such as beliefs in gods, ancestors, taboos, and afterlives rather than say, a given origin story or a sporting affiliation, and occupy nearly every terrestrial corner of the planet occupied by humans. One of the means by which religions communicate so well, it seems, is by individuals' emotional expressions.[31] The automatic, interpretable, and reliable qualities of emotions that Darwin recognised in identifying motivational states enabled people to predict what others would do. Moreover, experiences of fear—*trembling, which made all my bones to shake*—are particularly effective modalities of cooperative prediction because fear is such a powerful and

28. R Sosis, J Bulbulia, 'The behavioral ecology of religion: the benefits and costs of one evolutionary approach', in *Religion*, 41/3 (2011): 341–362. https://doi.org/10.1080/0048721X.2011.604514
29. W Irons, 'Why People Believe (What Other People See As) Crazy Ideas', in *The Evolution of Religion: Studies, Theories, and Critiques*, edited by J Bulbulia, R Sosis, R Genet, E Harris, K Wyman, & C Genet (Santa Margarita CA: Collins Foundation Press, 2008), 51–60.
30. R Sosis, & ER Bressler 'Cooperation and Commune Longevity: A Test of the Costly Signaling Theory of Religion', in *Cross-Cultural Research*, 37/2 (2003): 234.
31. J Bulbulia, 'The Cognitive and Evolutionary Psychology of Religion', in *Biology and Philosophy*, 18/5 (2004): 655–686. https://doi.org/10.1007/s10539-005-5568-6

important motivator and, not least, so clearly broadcast to everyone else as well. We next consider how fear, in a devotional setting, fosters cooperation.

The Logic of Fear in Religious Cultural Systems

A recurring feature in religious systems is a fear of punishment not from other fellow humans, but from supernatural agents or agency.[32] The form and details vary greatly, but the wrath of the gods or spirits crops up in numerous and potent ways across cultures and religions. Broad surveys of religions suggest that the role of punishment is by no means a special case of a few ancient, indigenous, or modern religions. Rather, it is common across the world's cultures and throughout history.[33] For example, in a purpose-built database of 116 Pacific religious cultures,[34] all but one culture had a tradition of supernatural punishment beliefs.[35]

The pattern appears to hold globally. In the 1940s, George Murdock catalogued the common features that existed across several

32. D Johnson, 'Why God is the Best Punisher', *Religion, Brain & Behavior*, 1/1 (2011): 77–84. https://doi.org/10.1080/2153599X.2011.558714; DDP Johnson, 'God's Punishment and Public Goods', in *Human Nature*, 16/4 (2005): 410–446. https://doi.org/10.1007/s12110-005-1017-0; FL Roes, & M Raymond, 'Belief in Moralizing Gods', in *Evolution and Human Behavior: Official Journal of the Human Behavior and Evolution Society*, 24/2 (2003): 126–135.
33. DDP Johnson, *God is Watching You: How the Fear of God Makes Us Human* (New York: Oxford University Press, 2016); A Norenzayan, *Big Gods: How Religion Transformed Cooperation and Conflict* (Princeton, NJ: Princeton University Press, 2013); BG Purzycki, C Apicella, QD Atkinson, E Cohen, RA McNamara, AK Willard, J Henrich 'Moralistic Gods, Supernatural Punishment and the Expansion of Human Sociality', in *Nature*, 530 (2016): 327–330; HB Earhart, *Religious Traditions of the World: A Journey Through Africa, Mesoamerica, North America, Judaism, Christianity, Islam, Hinduism, Buddhism, China, and Japan* (New York: HarperOne, 1992). https://ixtheo.de/Record/1613750102
34. For an interactive map of the distributions of Pacific religions, see: https://pulotu.shh.mpg.de/compare/.
35. J Watts, O Sheehan, SJ Greenhill, S Gomes-Ng, QD Atkinson, J Bulbulia, & RD Gray, (2015). 'Pulotu: Database of Austronesian Supernatural Beliefs and Practices', in *PloS One*, '/9 (2015), e0136783. https://doi.org/10.1371/journal.pone.0136783

hundred indigenous societies around the world.[36] This dataset has since been used to look explicitly at whether there is any empirical evidence that societies with gods that were more 'moralising' were also more cooperative.[37] Moralising gods were defined, following previous research in anthropology, as spiritual beings who are present and active in human affairs, and specifically supportive of human morality.[38] Across the whole sample, moralising gods were significantly more frequent among societies that were larger, more norm compliant (in some tests), loan and use abstract money, are centrally sanctioned, policed, and pay taxes. Inasmuch as moralizing gods are more likely to threaten negative consequences for those who disregard the norms of the community, this study provided support for the notion that supernatural punishment may indeed be an important promoter of cooperation among human societies. It certainly suggests that something is going on here in the link between religion and cooperation. Theories that hold that religion is an arbitrary by-product of big brains or culture do not predict any relationship between indices of cooperation and whether moralizing gods are present or not. More recent empirical studies corroborate a link between beliefs in supernatural punishment and levels of behavioural cooperation.[39]

Arguably, we should not be surprised by the recurrence of punishment, and the fear that punishment instils, in the numerous cultural systems and religions across the world and across time. As we have argued above, of the many signals humans (and other animals)

---

36. GP Murdock, 'The Common Denominator of Cultures', *Perspectives on Human Evolution*, edited by SL Washburn and PC Jay (New York: Holt, Rinehart and Winston, 1968), 230–245. https://opus4.kobv.de/opus4-Fromm/frontdoor/index/index/docId/17044
37. DDP Johnson, 'God's Punishment and Public Goods', in *Human Nature*, 16/4 (2005): 410–446. https://doi.org/10.1007/s12110-005-1017-0
38. GE Swanson, *The Birth of the Gods* (Ann Arbor: University of Michigan, 1960).
39. Purzycki, 'Moralistic Gods, Supernatural Punishment and the Expansion of Human Sociality'; AF Shariff, A Norenzayan, & J Henrich, 'The Birth of High Gods: How the Cultural Evolution of Supernatural Policing Agents Influenced the Emergence of Complex, Cooperative Human Societies, Paving the Way for Civilization', in *Evolution, Culture and the Human Mind*, edited by M Schaller, A Norenzayan, S Heine, T Yamagishi & T Kameda (New York: Psychology Press, 2009), 119–136. AF Shariff, A Norenzayan, 'Mean Gods Make Good People: Different Views of God Predict Cheating Behavior. *International Journal for the Psychology of Religion*, 21/2 (2011): 85–96

send and receive, perhaps the most powerful and the most important for survival and reproduction is fear.[40] Fear keeps us alive. It is critical to an organism's persistence in the face of competition and predation. Indeed, psychologists have identified a powerful psychological principle known as the 'negativity bias', which describes people's greater sensitivity to bad than good events (even if otherwise equivalent in magnitude). A wide-ranging review by Roy Baumeister and colleagues characterized the negativity bias as 'one of the most basic and far-reaching psychological principles'.[41] An independent review by Rozin and Royzman similarly argued the negativity bias was a 'general principle' that 'holds across a wide range of domains'.[42] A large number of experimental studies have confirmed and replicated the phenomenon of negativity bias in carefully controlled laboratory conditions, where positive and negative stimuli can be manipulated to be identical in frequency and magnitude, and other factors ruled out. Furthermore, neuroscientists have observed the brain reacting more strongly to negative stimuli than equivalent positive stimuli, again under experimentally controlled conditions.[43] Negative experiences have a special power over human thinking and behaviour.

The negativity bias is evident across a wide range of contexts. At perhaps the most fundamental level (harking back to Darwin's puzzle at the start), it is particularly notable among the six basic emotions that are universally displayed by all humans across cultures—happiness, surprise, disgust, sadness, fear, and anger. Only one is posi-

40. DT Blumstein, *The Nature of Fear: Survival Lessons from the Wild* (Harvard University Press 2020).
41. RF Baumeister, E Bratslavsky, C Finkenauer, & KD Vohs, 'Bad is Stronger than Good', in *Review of General Psychology: Journal of Division 1, of the American Psychological Association*, 5/4 (2001), 357.
42. P Rozin, & EB Royzman, 'Negativity Bias, Negativity Dominance, and Contagion', in *Personality and Social Psychology Review: An Official Journal of the Society for Personality and Social Psychology, Inc*, 5/4 (2001): 296–320. https://doi.org/10.1207/S15327957PSPR0504_2
43. TA Ito, JT Larsen, NK Smith, & JT Cacioppo (1998). 'Negative Information Weighs More Heavily on the Brain: The Negativity Bias in Evaluative Categorizations', in *Journal of Personality and Social Psychology*, 75/4 (1998): 887–900. https://doi.org/10.1037//0022-3514.75.4.887; NK Smith, JT Cacioppo, JT Larsen, & TL Chartrand, (2003). 'May I Have Your Attention, Please: Electrocortical Responses to Positive and Negative Stimuli', in *Neuropsychologia*, 41/2 (1998): 171–183. https://doi.org/10.1016/s0028-3932(02)00147-1

tive, whereas four are negative (the remaining one, surprise, can be either).[44] Other studies find that stress and a lack of social support can cause immune suppression, but positive alternatives (such as relaxation therapies and social support) do not provide equivalent benefits.[45] Meanwhile, phobias can arise after a single negative learning experience, but there is no comparable effect for positive experiences. More generally, among journalists and scholars of communication, 'it is considered common knowledge that bad events are more newsworthy and attract more reader attention'.[46] 'Over and over', as psychologist Jonathan Haidt summarized this school of research, 'the mind reacts to bad things more quickly, strongly and persistently than to equivalent good things'.[47]

But *why* do people have a negativity bias and how does this play out in connection with religion? Psychologists believe that this dominance of bad over good emerged as an adaptive trait to avoid lethal dangers in evolutionary history.[48] At first glance, a systematic misperception of the world seems to be counterproductive. However, fixating on bad things—in both perception and behaviour—is likely to have helped survival and reproductive success in ancestral environments. All organisms experience a fundamental asymmetry in which opportunities (positive events) may be welcome but are rarely vital, whereas dangers (negative events) can be a matter of life and death.[49] In an important sense, therefore, negative events are more important than positive events. Consequently, we would expect natural selection to favour dispositions that steer organisms away from peril.[50]

---

44. D Brown, *Human Universals* (New York: McGraw-Hill Companies, Incorporated, 1991). https://play.google.com/store/books/details?id=YQPFQgAACAAJ
45. Baumeister, 'Bad is Stronger than Good', 343.
46. Baumeister, 'Bad is Stronger than Good', 343.
47. Tony Schwartz, 'Overcoming Your Negativity Bias', in *New York Times* (14 June 2013) https://dealbook.nytimes.com/2013/06/14/overcoming-your-negativity-bias/.
48. Baumeister, 'Bad is Stronger than Good', 343.
49. D Kahneman, & E Patrick, *Thinking, Fast and Slow* (London: Penguin Books, 2011).
50. MG Haselton, & D Nettle, 'The Paranoid Optimist: An Integrative Evolutionary Model of Cognitive Biases', *Personality and Social Psychology Review: An Official Journal of the Society for Personality and Social Psychology, Inc*, 10/1 (2006): 47–66. https://doi.org/10.1207/s15327957pspr1001_3

This is precisely what we observe. A hair-trigger sensitivity to threat and the 'fight or flight' response are widely evident across all mammals as well as other taxonomic groups, and arise in humans via the release of adrenaline even before people fully perceive the source of the stimulus.[51] Fear is a deeply entrenched part of human nature. But in fact it is way deeper than that—comprising biological mechanisms that we share with many other organisms stretching back far into our history. As Dan Blumstein put it, 'Over millions of years fear has kept our ancestors alive—not only our human ancestors but our nonhuman ancestors too'.[52] Fear has evidently been a key trait of the survivors. What is critical is to recognise that, over evolutionary time, many *social* phenomena have developed to harness these same underlying *somatic* responses. 'When social threats arise', as Blumstein explains, 'they engage some of the same physiological and psychological systems that previously ensured safety from predators'.[53]

Let us return to the question we posed at the outset: What is it about religious expression that religious commitment communicates, in a manner that is automatic and hard to fake? The answer is that religious behaviour communicates a motivational response to an authority that is higher than oneself. As Job asked: *Shall mortal man be more just than God? Shall a man be more pure than his Maker?* Job's fear and trembling reveals that he is humbled before a higher power. Though not all religions adopt a terrifying image of the gods, most religions evoke experiences of reverence and piety directed to a restraining power.[54] And the ethnographic and psychological evidence above reveal that commitment to a morally 'policing' (or at least interested) authority is commonplace. It is through a person's morphological expressions that we learn something important to our own interests about Job's psychological and motivational state: Job is humbled before God. And once we understand Job's psychological

51. R McDermott, 'The Feeling of Rationality: The Meaning of Neuroscientific Advances for Political Science', in *Perspectives on Politics*, 2/4 (2004): 691–706. http://www.jstor.org/stable/3688538
52. Blumstein, *The Nature of Fear*, 343.
53. Blumstein, *The Nature of Fear*, 343.
54. Johnson, *God is Watching You*, HL Lenfesty, & TJH Morgan, 'By Reverence, Not Fear: Prestige, Religion, and Autonomic Regulation in the Evolution of Cooperation', in *Frontiers in Psychology*, 10 (2019): 2750. https://doi.org/10.3389/fpsyg.2019.02750, Norenzayan, *Big Gods*.

and motivational states we can predict his actions (with mutual benefits to all actors). Job will likely restrain himself in accordance with his beliefs in God's justice. Such predictability only works, however, if Job's emotions are automated, readily interpretable to strangers, and reliably linked to his psychological and motivational states in a manner that is not under Job's control. That is what natural selection deemed effective as well.

Cultures of Fear: Part of the Problem and Part of the Solution

To summarise the story so far, we have seen that emotions evolved not merely as internal springs and restraints on action, but as prophets that broadcast emotional states to an audience of others in a manner that cannot easily be feigned. Emotions are prophetic because they predict behaviours. They are reliable prophets because their expression is automatic and hard to fake. Whereas language is arbitrary, one can say 'the check is in the mail' even when it is not, emotions are indexical and reflexive. When fear overwhelms, we shudder. Others may even shudder too, not necessarily because they see what we fear themselves, but because they fear whatever it is that we evidently fear. Communication evolved to be indexical because cooperative dilemmas can only effectively be solved when organisms are somewhat predictable and do not lie.[55]

There is an emerging consensus that among humans, religious beliefs and behaviours developed at least in part because such beliefs enabled religious agents to predict each other's cooperative behaviours—and better than they could do so without those religious commitments and signals.[56] Because incentives to cheat arise throughout the myriad forms of social interaction, emotions triggered by religious beliefs, and in particular fear invoked by beliefs about religious agents and imperatives, serve as social expressions that are hard to fake and are imprinted on the faces and behaviours of believers.

55. For a discussion of how communication evolves in predator prey interactions and this connection to religion see: J Bulbulia, 'The Cognitive and Evolutionary Psychology of Religion', in *Biology and Philosophy*, 18/5 (2004): 655–686. https://doi.org/10.1007/s10539-005-5568-6

56. K Sterelny, 'Religion Re-explained', in *Religion, Brain & Behavior*, 8/4 (2018): 406–425. https://doi.org/10.1080/2153599X.2017.1323779

Religions are one powerful catalyst for such emotional expressions—sometimes explicitly in public settings. There is much more to say about the evolution of emotions such as fear, and how this was manifested in, and captured by, religions and their rituals, practices, and belief systems. With the emergence of large-scale societies in particular, religion became transformed. It was no longer sufficient to observe the piety of individuals because humans in large societies regularly transact with strangers.[57] Was this stranger wearing a cross a true believer and norm follower? More public acts of commitment and ritual participation would be needed to advertise and verify group belonging and loyalty. However, our point here has been a simpler one, to clarify that emotions such as fear have adaptive functions, and that the mechanisms of such emotions, fear in particular, have been leveraged for cooperation. The evolutionary logic of fear reveals a pathway not only to social cooperation but also to a broader social justice, something that did not feature in Bonhoeffer's sermon, and is indeed readily overlooked. In political theatre, fear is part of the problem, rather than a guarantor of social harmony. For one thing, most obviously, it can easily be manipulated for nefarious ends, however useful its intended function may have been in evolution's eye. However, in many other instances of *religious* theatre, when fear is channelled through piety, reverence, and devotion, fear can be part of the solution—an engine that drives up levels of cooperation and group cohesion to levels that would scarcely be possible without it.[58] As society scaled up, however, and politics rose above and ultimately divorced from church, the efficacy or stability of fear's good effects have often become stretched very thin.

Before concluding, it might be objected that Bonhoeffer was interested in cultures in a state of 'chronic' fear and anxiety, rather than sudden hair-raising experiences of 'acute' fear, such as encountering an SS officer. However, the two states are linked. Darwin introduced the passage from Job in our epigraph by writing, 'Of vague fear there is a well-known and grand description in Job:—"In thoughts from the visions of the night" . . .'[59] Darwin's *Expression of Emotions* hoped

57. J Bulbulia, 'Spreading Order: Religion, Cooperative Niche Construction, and Risky Coordination Problems', in *Biology & Philosophy*, 27/1 (2012): 1–27. https://doi.org/10.1007/s10539-011-9295-x

58. Lenfesty, & Morgan, 'By Reverence, Not Fear'.

59. Darwin, *The Expression of the Emotions in Man and Animals*, 291.

to describe 'diversified expressions of fear, in its gradations from mere attention to a start of surprise, into extreme terror and horror.'[60] Although we focused on Darwin's discussion of extreme fear states, his *Expression of Emotions* is committed to a continuity of embodied affective states in a variety of manifestations. The passage from Job illustrates that the continuum of emotional states are not fixed. A culture of chronic fear is one in which bodies are primed to act, or become sensitized to act, in accordance with basic emotions. Where the culture is widespread, responses become predictable, precisely because of the underlying biological triggers and reactions. In more 'natural' settings where emotions effectively help to regulate pro-social behaviour, the effects of such cultures may be mutually benefiting. We might wish to live in a culture in which people fear breaching good relations with divinity, because in such a culture, where divine ideals align with justice, people will be (or should approximate to being) predictably just.[61]

Conclusions

In his speech in Berlin in 1933, Bonhoeffer chided people not to be fearful of the political turmoil and rise of the Nazis. He told stories from the Bible to illustrate how fear can often be unfounded as well as debilitating in the face of danger and uncertainty, and that we must cast fear aside and be faithful instead. Only this could avert disaster. Facing up to the source of our fear can help us to eliminate it rather than suffer it.

Bonhoeffer made a vitally important observation. Maybe if people had been less fearful—citizens and opinion leaders in Germany as well as political leaders abroad—Hitler could have been stopped

60. Darwin, *The Expression of the Emotions in Man and Animals*, 307.

61. Of course, there are differences in some conditions brought about by acute and chronic experiences of fear. For example, psychologists have found that, when both animals and people suffer ongoing punishment yet they have no control over their situation, they fall into a state of 'learned helplessness' in which they become depressed and unresponsive—even missing opportunities to help themselves out of the situation See MEP Seligman, 'Learned Helplessness', *Annual Review of Medicine*, 23/1 (1972):407-412. Trauma and post-traumatic stress disorder can similarly lead to states of chronically depressed mood. These normally occur after recurrent and/or sustained exposure to a source of fear.

earlier. But on the other hand, given what was to come and the lack of other people shedding their fear themselves, maybe fear was for many the only recourse and guide for action, at least for individuals who would have suffered lethal consequences (for themselves and others) of standing up to a brutal regime.

So how do we make sense of when fear helps or hurts us in such complex social phenomena? It clearly cuts both ways. First of all, an evolutionary point of view reminds us that fear is not necessarily a detriment or barrier that undermines our wellbeing. Instead, it is at its most fundamental level an adaptive trait that tells us when to run, hide, or avoid drawing attention—even or especially when our rational brains might want us to do the opposite. Fear is a powerful and important strategic instinct that is often desirable and sometimes essential, and maybe even saves us from actions that might lead to disaster. That is, after all, why evolution found it necessary to wire up our bodies specifically to overwhelm our normal, calm and calculating selves, literally bypassing our brains to enable rapid fight, flight, or freezing mechanisms when they are needed.

This adaptive advantage of fear is hardly unique to humans, but rather universally recurrent across a wide range of taxonomic groups in the animal kingdom, speaking to its power and success. Indeed, the negativity bias suggests that fear even has a special leverage over positive events of a similar magnitude, meaning that we should expect fear and other negative emotions to play a greater role than 'nicer' emotions and events in many social phenomena of importance.

Even amidst the great complexity of religion, where Bonhoeffer started, fear turns out to have a critical theoretical and empirical role in promoting compliance and cooperation—precisely because it taps into such a deep-seated human biology associated with fear and its responses. But in addition, fear works its magic even at the level of social problems. In several recent empirical studies, punishment (and supernatural punishment in particular) appears to be remarkably effective at deterring cheats and free-riders.[62] When it comes to instances of social discord and human evil, fear and elite manipulation of fear has not infrequently been part of the problem, but they have also been, and may still yet be, an important part of the solution.

62. Y Hartberg, M Cox, & S Villamayor-Tomas, 'Supernatural Monitoring and Sanctioning in Community-based Resource Management', in *Religion, Brain & Behavior*, 6/2 (2016): 95–111.

The evolutionary logic of fear stresses that it is automatic. It cannot be willed away. However, it can be supplemented or supplanted by awe. The evolutionary logic of *religion* reveals that the cultivation of reverence of sacred authority—though often anchored in the hair-raising experiences of a sublime creator deity—was among the innovations that transformed humans into super-cooperators.[63]

To end, while Bonhoeffer warned us of the dangers of fear, we suggest that in broader context fear can also be seen as a highly adaptive evolutionary trait. It is of course contingent, sometimes arising in ways that hurt us instead of helping us, and often benefiting those who exploit it rather than those who experience it. But, either way, like hunger and love, it is an instinct that helps us make important life choices. The tragedy is that, given the pitfalls of 'evolutionary mismatch', where our evolved behaviours become victims to evolutionarily novel circumstances and scales of political organisation for which we were never prepared, fear can lead to spectacular disasters, not least clearing the way for Hitler's willing executioners. Bonhoeffer stands out because, unlike so many others, he was not afraid to speak out.

63. Lenfesty, & Morgan, 'By Reverence, Not Fear'.

Vol 7 No 1&2/2019

Bonhoeffer Navigating a Way Through Law, Justice, and Faith

Karola Radler

Introduction

When in early March 1940[1] Bonhoeffer mentioned in his letter to the professor of constitutional law Gerhard Leibholz an unfinished conversation, he did not just refer to an episode during his stay-over with his friend and relative in England on his return-trip from New York in September 1939.[2] Rather Bonhoeffer referred to an old discourse—'an old topic of discussion'—which stretches back to the 1920s and became fundamental to his book on *Ethics*,[3] the chapters of which he began to write and assemble in late 1940.

A rare insight into the depth of their friendship can be found in Leibholz' *Memoir* which he published in the 1948 first edition to Bonhoeffer's *The Cost of Discipleship*.[4] Their first intellectual interaction can be positively traced to their respective *habilitation* theses, both written in the late 1920s when their residency in Berlin overlapped. Both had approached from their respective paradigms of thought and from opposing phenomenological perspectives the 'question of consciousness and conscience'.[5] Bonhoeffer declared in his thesis on *Act and Being*[6] that God's revelation goes beyond philosophical concepts

1. DBWE (Dietrich Bonhoeffer Works English) 15:300–3; DBW (Dietrich Bonhoeffer Werke) 15: *Illegale Theologenausbildung: Sammelvikariate 1937–1940* [Theological education underground: 1937–1940], edited by Dirk Schulz (Gütersloh: Kaiser/ Gütersloher Verlagshaus, 1998), 296–300.
2. DBWE 17:93. Bonhoeffer stayed with the Leibholz family from 13–25 July 1939.
3. DBWE 6.
4. Dietrich Bonhoeffer, *The Cost of Discipleship* (London: SCM Press, 1948).
5. DBWE 10:122.
6. DBWE 2.

of knowledge which close the human being in on the self, including decision-makers. Leibholz, in his *Habilitation* thesis on *The Essence of Representation*,[7] attempted to prove that the parliamentary representative and legislative decision maker[8] 'bundled . . . the spiritual essence in himself', that is, 'the ability to know *a priori*, supra-temporal concepts of state-theory.[9]

At its core the March 1940 letter asks if principles of law can possibly claim absolute validity within creation and further whether there was a potential cohesive relationship between law, justice, and love. More specifically, Bonhoeffer claims that, law, justice, and love in the sense of the Sermon on the Mount belong together, despite being antithesis. Their relation hinges on the interconnection of history and revelation, on creation and redemption. For determining whether there are indeed absolute principles of law within creation is decisive whether the focus is placed on factual power or divine scripture. The result would either be a relativisation of revelation or the relativisation of the historical, i. e. the norms of creation. The underlying difference between law of creation, which connects to questions of *jus naturale, lex naturae*, and law within redemption Bonhoeffer suggests resolving with an understanding of law as oriented toward justice. Then, despite being a historical reality and strictly enforceable through power, law is not an abstract idea, but Christian love in the sense of "the pedagogue leading up to Christ" (Gal. 3:24). Law on earth thus warrants the possibility of actually proclaiming Christian love. Never becoming identical, law and love maintain their antith-

7. Gerhard Leibholz, *Das Wesen der Repräsentation unter besonderer Berücksichtigung des Repräsentativsystems: Ein Beitrag zur allgemeinen Staats- und Verfassungslehre* [The essence of representation under special consideration of the system of representation: A contribution to the general theory of law and constitution], Beiträge zum ausländischen öffentlichen Recht und Völkerrecht 13 (Berlin: de Gruyter, 1929); Cited below as *Repräsentation.*
8. Article 21 of the 1919 Weimar Constitution demanded of parliamentary representatives a submission to their conscience; Horst Hildebrandt, editor, *Die deutschen Verfassungen des 19. und 20. Jahrhunderts* [The German constitutions of the 19th and 20th centuries], 11th enlarged edition (Paderborn: Ferdinand Schöningh, 1979), 75.
9. Gerhard Leibholz, *Das Wesen der Repräsentation und der Gestaltwandel der Demokratie im 20. Jahrhundert* [The essence of representation and the changes to the form of democracy in the 20th century], 2nd extended edition (Berlin: Walter de Gruyter, 1960), 19; Cited below as *Repräsentation und Gestaltwandel.*

esis. As holy justice and love from God, the judge, it is gifted out of His Grace and revealed in the cross. This justice "before God" means submission to God and must be strictly distinguished from the Aristotelian concept of justice as well as from justice in the sense of *suum cuique*.

The Bonhoeffer—Leibholz discourse attaches to the intellectual controversies regarding methods and direction (*Methoden—und Richtungsstreit*) that ensued in the early twentieth century.[10] As a political consequence to the 1919 Weimar Constitution, which had established a juristic positive legitimacy for the first German republic, ensued in the jurisprudential academy a discourse on positivism, on processes of decision-making, on legal oversight, and most of all on problems of legal calculability and security (*Rechtssicherheit*). And within the theological paradigm of thought engaging with juristic terms had become necessary due to the constitutional novelty of the prohibition of a state-church[11] and the resulting need in the Lutheran Church for restructuring its financial and internal organization independently of the state.

This paper is concerned with the question inasmuch in the context of their time the theologian Bonhoeffer's interaction with the jurist Leibholz can clarify the interconnection and differences the terms legislated law (*Gesetz*), law as rights (*Recht*) and justice (*Gerechtigkeit*)[12] denote, especially in the sense of claims to absoluteness, and inasmuch they relate to Bonhoeffer's theological understanding of love. The investigation will be streamlined[13] by focusing on the early twen-

10. Manfred Friedrich, 'Der Methoden- und Richtungsstreit: Zur Grundlagendiskussion der Weimarer Staatsrechtslehre' [The controversy on method and direction: The foundational discourse of the Weimar theory of state], in *Archiv des öffentlichen Rechts*, 102/2 (1977): 161–209.

11. Article 137 Weimar Constitution; Hildebrandt, *Die deutschen Verfassungen*, 102.

12. The official English translation of Bonhoeffer's work uses for the German word *Gerechtigkeit* mostly, but inconsistently, the term 'righteousness' which is foremost associated with the theological paradigm. However, the term *Gerechtigkeit* pertains also to the jurisprudential paradigm. Therefore, I translate this term as 'justice' in relation to both intellectual discourses.

13. For the purpose of keeping the focus of this article on the interaction between Bonhoeffer's theology and Leibholz's jurisprudence I excluded from this paper such references in Bonhoeffer's 1940 letter which denote specific theological connections such as to Barth's and Brunner's theology as well as to Hegel's idealism and Trölsch's understanding of natural law.

tieth century's interest in establishing for theology as well as for the legal science of jurisprudence (*Rechtswissenschaft*) independent academic spheres and the resulting far–reaching consequences.

The Question of Law (*Rechtsfrage*):

The question of law, the juristic question, the *Rechtsfrage*, as Kant would call it, is that of mediation, of healing, as a consequence of the individual's discovery of the self's intellect apart from a surrounding world. In a process of secularisation the spheres of transcendence and immanence separated and led to a polyphony[14] of dichotomies such as object and subject, private and public, office and person, formal and substantial, legality and legitimacy. Divinely ordained natural law became in the course of scientific discoveries the law of nature which turned the perception of human beings from simply being human to possessing a human nature. Theologically determined truth, *veritas*, became secularised will, *voluntas*, and in an attempt of finding common ground between mediaeval fragmented localised legal traditions, authority-based Roman law, the *ius positivum*, became increasingly received as part of the legal understanding.[15] And in a context of weakening divine certainty and theological authority, Roman law could be used as political instrument for as well as against political absolutism, that is, as either giving authority or as limiting powers through subjugating everything physical under the law of nature expressed in *ius positivum*. Increasingly legal norms served secularised human temporal purpose and history contested

14. By using the term polyphony is meant that a multitude of overlapping dichotomies nonetheless play the same tune of Modernity. Further dichotomies are: God—individual, above—below, fiction—fact, theory—praxis, meta-norm—reality, *a priori—a posteriori*, idea—fact, profession—family, and others.
15. Michael Stolleis, 'The Legitimation of Law through God, tradition, will, nature, and constitution', in *Natural Law and Laws of Nature in Early Modern Europe: Jurisprudence, Theology, Moral and Natural Philosophy*, edited by Lorraine Daston and Michael Stolleis (Burlington: Ashgate, 2008), 47. The cannon law of the Catholic Church was originally understood as given by God the creator of nature and therefore as *ius naturale* (natural law) being in harmony with *ius divinum* (divine law). Therefore the Catholic Church's *ius positivum* (positive or written law) could still be amended to comply with the *ius naturale* (natural law) which led to understanding the written Catholic canon law as derived from *ius divinum* (divine law).

all theories of natural law. In idealist theory human beings, carried by individual determination, strived towards this-worldly perfection until it fuses with the divine. And historicism's refusal of recognizing a logical necessity in human nature affirmed that human beings had not nature but history which, in turn, relativised all that what previously could be understood as absolute and as the legitimizing foundation for law.

With the insight of the relative conditioning of all order came the problem of legitimizing the highest unit for decisions within a historical particular order. In the early nineteenth century a compromise that differentiated between the "substance" and the "application" of power identified the state as the highest third, the sovereign, which would mediate between the princes and the estates (*Stände*).[16] The opposing natural law universalisms that reappeared in this question of sovereignty either being carried from below or from above was solved by hypostasizing the state to a meta-individual, a juristic person, and the highest and last idea of life. However, a strengthening bourgeois class in Germany, committed to the ideas of the 1789 French Revolution, insisted on an intensified reception of Roman law in the form of codified law. This class of learned lawyers and masters of a by now specialised language[17] was committed to limiting the state's objective of power through dissolving power into pure relations of contractual will by tying norms to formal normative attributions (*Zurechnungen*). The crowning success for this Romanist school

16. Christian Graf von Krochow, *Die Entscheidung: eine Untersuchung* über *Ernst Jünger, Carl Schmitt, Martin Heidegger* [The decision: an investigation into Ernst Jünger, Carl Schmitt, Martin Heidegger] (Frankfurt/ Main: Campus, 1990), 22–23. This compromise was reached at the end of the Napoleonic wars at the 1815 Congress of Vienna under the Austrian Count Metternich. It attempted to reorganise Europe through balancing the powers of the European countries and their princes. This system succeeded in bringing relative peace to Europe until the Industrial Revolution in the second half of the nineteenth century led to increased economic competition between the countries which gave rise to nationalism throughout Europe. The increasing international tensions found their outlet in the 1914 First World War.

17. Especially a group of professors from Berlin insisted on adding to the (unsuccessful) 1848 Frankfurt *Paulskirchen* (St Paul's Church) Constitution a written list of basic rights; Friedrich Ebel and Georg Thielmann, *Rechtsgeschichte: Von der Römischen Antike bis zur Neuzeit* [History of law: From Roman antiquity to Modernity] (Heidelberg: CF Müller, 2003), 334, 336, 340–43.

of thought, based on the *corpus iuris civilis*, was the 1900 Civil Code which secured over against the ruling authority (*Obrigkeit*) a private space of contractual freedoms for economic pursuits and at the same time unified local practices of law (*Gewohnheitsrecht*). Also, this development paralleled the political nationalist-driven unification of the German countries into the constitution-based monarchy of the 1871 German Reich.

In result the Romanist—Germanist discourse of the nineteenth century, mainly driven at opposing ends by the so called "Goethe of jurisprudence" Friedrich Carl von Savigny[18] on the Romanist side and the Germanist position which Otto von Gierke took in his 1868 *Genossenschaftsrecht*,[19] led to recognising legislated law (*Gesetz*) as the only source of law (*Recht*).[20] This idea of legal positivism and abstract normativism in which there are only valid norms cast into "non-ruling" statutes Hans Kelsen organised into a system of logical deductions within a hierarchy of statutes and with the constitutional text, such as the 1919 Weimar Constitution, serving as legitimizing hypothesis of origin.[21] This abstract system that disempowers the state by identifying the source of law (*Recht*) with the state and the state with law as *Gesetz*, promised legal security over against actions taken by the state. However, deprived of substance and explanations this calculability could reverse into pure arbitrariness on part of the authorities. Consequently, by the early 1920s the *Rechtsfrage*, now cast into bourgeois-liberal constitutional form, concerned the ques-

18. Joachim Ruckert, 'Friedrich Carl von Savigny, the legal method, and the Modernity of law', in *Juridica International*, 11 (2006): 55–67. Ebel and Thielmann, *Rechtsgeschichte*, 328.
19. Otto von Gierke, *Deutsches Genossenschaftsrecht* [German law of cooperatives], volume 1: *Rechtsgeschichte der deutschen Genossenschaft* [History of law of the German cooperative] (Berlin: Weidmann'sche Buchhandlung, 1868).
20. For Paul Laband law (*Recht*) is that which is legislated law (*Gesetz*), that is, what was promulgated in a formal process. Paul Laband, *Das Staatsrecht des Deutschen Reiches* [The theory of state of the German Reich], 5th edition (Tübingen: Mohr Siebeck, 1913).
21. Hans Kelsen, *Die philosophischen Grundlagen der Naturrechtslehre und des Rechtspositivismus* [The philosophical foundations of the theory of natural law and positivism of law], Philosophische Vorträge 31 (Charlottenburg 2: Pan-Verlag Rolf Heise, 1928); Same, *Introduction to the Problems of Legal Theory*, translated by Bonnie Litschewski Paulson and Stanley L Paulson (Oxford: Clarendon Press, 1992).

tion of overcoming abstractness by connecting "pure" thinking with a lived factual reality (*Wirklichkeit*) in which criteria of objectivity had dissolved and subjectivity struggled with uncertainty.

The Bonhoeffer-Leibholz Discourse

By 1940 the National Socialist regime was well into implementing article 19 of their program[22] which called for reversing the reception of Roman law and replacing this Christian-Roman tradition[23] with a decisively German "community law" (*Gemeinschaftsrecht*) that was geared towards uniting in one human decision-maker legitimacy, legality, final jurisdiction over all life, and also faith. This not only obliterated the democratic division of powers of the 1919 Weimar Constitution but also destroyed the liberal basic freedoms that were based on will and were grounded during the bourgeois fights of the nineteenth century in an increasing distance between a private and a public space.[24] A renaissance of Gierke's protest against the Civil Code[25] ensued and the juristic person of the state was replaced with a universal, all-encompassing, and all-pervading community that demanded faith in a totality that was built on leadership and followers.[26] Savigny's historic school of thought within law was accused and discredited by the jurist Carl Schmitt as having replaced the '*ius natu-*

22. Peter Landau, ‚Römisches Recht und deutsches Gemeinrecht'[Roman law and German common law], in *Rechtsgeschichte im Nationalsozialismus: Beiträge zur Geschichte einer Disziplin* [History of law under Nationalsocialism: Contributions to the history of a discipline], edited by Michael Stolleis and Dieter Simon (Tübingen: Mohr Siebeck, 1989).
23. Ville Suuronen, 'Mobilizing the Western tradition for present politics: Carl Schmitt's polemical uses of Roman law, 1923–1945', in *History of European Ideas* (2020), 10 at <DOI:10.1080/01916599.2020.1818115>.
24. Ernst Rudolf Huber, Einheit und Gliederung des völkischen Rechts: Ein Beitrag zur Überwindung des Gegensatzes von öffentlichem Recht und privatem Recht [Unity and structure of populist law: A contribution to overcoming the contradiction of public law and private law], in *Zeitschrift für die gesamte Staatswissenschaft–ZgStW,* 98/2 (1938): 310–58. Michael Stolleis, *A History of Public Law in Germany 1914–1945*, translated by Thomas Dunlap (Oxford: Oxford University Press, 2004), 258–62.
25. Pierre Friedrich, 'Gierkes Protest gegen das BGB: Justitia—Italia oder Germania?' [Gierke's protest against the Civil Code: Justicia—Italia or Germania?], in *The Legal History Review,* 85 (2017): 325–61.
26. Stolleis, *History of Public Law*, 359.

rale of the preceding generations' with positivist ideas such as distributed by Kelsen.[27] However, also Kelsen had rejected the dualism of public and private law.[28] And Kelsen's positivism and Schmitt's decisionism, respectively based on an absolute state of law or a dictatorship, both dissolve any substance of value when faced with the force of facts and are only differentiated by Schmitt having dropped positivism's foundational fiction of the idea of a rule by law (*Rechtsidee*).[29]

Any defenders of Roman law's separations, abstractions, and lines of authority came immediately under suspicion. Nonetheless, defenders took recourse to declaring that the older, classical Roman law had always been community bound.[30] Particularly contested were the Roman Ulpian's fundamental three precepts for law (*tria praecepta iuris*) as they had been handed down in the Digests and the Justinian Institutions: *honeste vivere, alterum non laedere, suum cuique tribuere* (live honest, do not harm others, render to each his own) and his definition of justice as 'constant and perpetual will of giving each his own right'.[31] The jurist Carl Schmitt took the battle against Roman law and liberalism in the years from 1933 to 1936 to particular extremes by declaring to free Germany from 'spiritual subjugation' under foreign systems of thought[32] implemented by an estate of Jewish lawyers.[33] He targeted especially Gerhard Leibholz who was a baptised Lutheran Christian of Jewish parents and with whom Schmitt had entertained close collegial and partly personal contact until April 1933.[34]

27. Carl Schmitt, 'Die Lage der europäischen Rechtswissenschaft' [The situation of the European science of law], in *Verfassungsrechtliche Aufsätze aus den Jahren 1924–1954* [Constitutional essays from the years 1924–1954], 386–429 (Berlin: Duncker & Humblot, 2003), 397–98, 402.
28. Stolleis, *History of Public Law*, 359.
29. Krochow, *Die Entscheidung*, 65–66.
30. Stolleis, *History of Public Law*, 360.
31. Ulpian defined justice as '*constans et perpetus voluntas jus suum cuique tribuendi*'. However, the expression *suum cuique tribuare* is often also attributed to Cicero and even further back to the Greek foundations in Plato and Aristotle; Marko Petrak, 'Plato and Ulpian's *Praecepta Iuris*', in *Fundamina*, 20/2 (2014): 697, 699.
32. Carl Schmitt, 'Die Logik der geistigen Unterwerfung' [The logic of intellectual submission], in *Deutsches Volkstum* (1934): 177–82.
33. Suuronen, 'Mobilizing', 12.
34. Karola Radler, 'The Leibholz—Schmitt connection's formative influence on Bonhoeffer's 1932–33 entry into public theology', in *Stellenbosch Theological Journal*, 4/2 (2018): 683–702.

Leibholz's Jurisprudential Position

Leibholz's jurisprudential theses[35] of the 1920s captures the signs of his time. He argues for claimable subjective basic rights with additional judicial oversight of the legislative institutions, for defining "equality before the law" in a way that limits arbitrary discretion on the part of the state (*Willkürverbot*), and searches for the material content of constitutional norms from an anti-positivist perspective that is foremost directed against Kelsen's mathematical logic.[36] He rejects natural law as well as a value-free formalism that eliminates valuable substantial elements and he supports the inclusion of teleological and sociological perspectives that he sees oriented on a reality which is by necessity political. For the purpose of connecting constitutional norms, especially equality, to the actual real world he differentiates between legal idea (*Rechtsidee*), legal concept (*Rechtsbegriff*), and legal ideal (*Rechtsideal*) and develops a method of directly viewing essences (*Wesensschau*). This method was meant to detect the actual, consolidated substance of constitutional institutes, especially that of the representation of ideas,[37] but should not be confused with ideological justifications.[38] This endeavor finds a similarity in Schmitt's 1912 pursuit of legal security by way of developing a method that would establish the correctness of decisions rendered by a judge who is situated between the legislated statute law (*Gesetz*) and juristic judgements (*Urteil*).[39] But in the final consequence it differs from Schmitt's decisionism which not just mediates but "heals" the

35. Gerhard Leibholz, *Die Gleichheit vor dem Gesetz: Eine Studie auf rechtsvergleichender und rechtsphilosophischer Grundlage* [Equality before the law: A study based on comparisons of law and philosophy of law], 2nd extended edition (Munich: CH Beck'sche Verlagsbuchhandlung, 1959), first published in 1925 by Otto Liebermann (Berlin). Leibholz, *Repräsentation.*
36. Gerhard Leibholz, 'Zur Begriffsbildung im öffentlichen Recht' [The conceptual formation in public law] (1931), in *Strukturprobleme der modernen Demokratie* [Structural problems of Modern democracy], 162-76, 3rd extended edition (Karlsruhe: CF Müller, 1967), 263.
37. Manfred Wiegandt, *Norm und Wirklickeit, Gerhard Leibholz (1901–1982)—Leben, Werk, und Richteramt* [Norm and reality, Gerhard Leibholz (1901–1982)—Life, work, and judicial office] (Baden-Baden: Nomos, 1995), 89.
38. Leibholz, *Repräsentation und Gestaltwandel*, 16.
39. Carl Schmitt, *Gesetz und Urteil: Eine Untersuchung zum Problem der Rechtspraxis* [Statute law and judgement: An investigation into the practice of law], 2nd edition (Munich: CH Beck, 1969; reprint 2009), first published in 1912.

moment of indifferent 'nothingness'[40] between law and decision with a human personification of ideas and hypostasising sovereign judgements *ex nihilo*.[41]

In his endeavor of clarifying "equality before the law" (*Gesetz*) Leibholz states that the judgement (*Urteil*) of calling a legal system correct necessitates a substantial concept of justice (*Gerechtigkeit*) which always already includes a value judgement and an idea of its form.[42] For this purpose he draws on distinctions between laws that contain rights (*Rechtsidee*), a system of laws (*Gesetze*), and ideals of law (*Rechtsideal*) such as justice. He refuses 'to discuss the uncountable theological, jurisprudential, or ethical attempts for defining the concept of justice'[43] because he considers it impossible to fixate a content that builds an inseparable unit with life itself. In substantiating his anti-positivism Leibholz explains that it was impossible to fixate *apriori* value in the concrete reality of a formal logical system of laws because of the inexhaustible multitude of tensions that continually developing facts present to idea and content.[44] Absolute judgements of value and a hierarchy of laws (*Gesetz*) are impossible because this would presuppose that values with fixed content exist and function as the basis for legal evaluations of juristic material. Rather it was the perpetual task of law (*Recht*) to strive to eliminate its distance to the ideal (*Rechtsideal*) of justice.[45] This correlation between the positive norm and justice which unequivocally connects "equality before the law" to justice, demands a substantial and not simply a formal concept of justice. However, because for Leibholz, unchangeable theorems or norms of timeless valid proportions, as natural law endeavors to evidence, are impossible, he refers to Kant's critical philosophy and the historical school's focus on knowledge's connection to concrete actualities.[46] Nonetheless, his objection to natural law's claim to abso-

40. Carl Schmitt, *Political Theology: Four Chapters on the Concept of Sovereignty*, translated by Georg Schwab (Chicago: University of Chicago Press, 2005), originally published in 1922 as *Politische Theologie: Vier Kapitel zur Lehre von der Souveränität* by Duncker & Humblot (Munich), 30.
41. Carl Schmitt, *Political Theology*, 32, 52.
42. Leibholz, *Gleichheit*, 55.
43. Leibholz, *Gleichheit*, 58 (own translation).
44. Leibholz, *Gleichheit*, 59, 67.
45. Leibholz, *Gleichheit*, 61.
46. Leibholz, *Gleichheit*, 60.

lutes is not absolute because he also rejects relativizing value within history.[47] He clarifies that he understands the idea of law (*Rechtsidee*) as absolute in the sense of absolutizing the changeability of relative content.[48]

According to Leibholz, an absolute value-judgement on just and unjust cannot be made on the basis of natural law.[49] Instead an allowance must be made for the Aristotelian proportionate concept of "equality" in the sense of *suum cuique*.[50] With referencing not Ulpian's but Aristotle's teaching for a definition of justice Leibholz evades the political discourse connected to Roman law[51] and lets him, nonetheless, use *suum cuique* in the sense of just distribution. It permits making use of Aristotle's logic, his dual purposes of allocation and compensation, and seeing justice as depending on equality.[52] But in difference to Aristotle who thought further criteria were necessary for determining justice and equality, Leibholz sees criteria as diluting with a multitude of exceptions the eligibility of a law formulated in general terms.[53] Thus he simply states that inherent to a just concept of equality are any differences between human beings insofar as their dissimilarities (*Ungleichartigkeiten*) are taken into account.[54] Concluding that as equal can be treated only what is in reality equal[55] he proceeds to limit the administrative, judicial, and especially legislative powers of discretion by defining equality at its minimum as

47. Leibholz, *Gleichheit*, 88.
48. Leibholz, *Gleichheit*, 60.
49. Leibholz's assessment of natural law in relation to positive law and constitutions goes back to his philosophical dissertation on Fichte; Gerhard Leibholz, *Fichte und der demokratische Gedanke: Ein Beitrag zur Staatslehre* [Fichte and the democratic thought: A contribution to the theory of state] (Freiburg: Julian Boltze, 1921).
50. Gerhard Leibholz, 'The foundations of justice and law in the light of the present European crisis' (1942), in *Politics and Law*, 253-270 (Leyden: Sythoff, 1965), 263.
51. Even though Leibholz discusses Aristotle it was Ulpian who 'transformed a Greek philosophical concept into a specifically legal concept'. Petrak, 'Plato and Ulpian's *Praecepta Iuris*', 699.
52. Hans Reiner, 'Die Hauptgrundlagen der fundamentalsten Normen der Naturrechts' [The main grounds of the most fundamental norms of natural law], in *Archiv für Rechts- und Sozialphilosophie*, 69/1 (1983): 2.
53. See to this Wiegandt, *Norm und Wirklickeit*, 104–5.
54. Leibholz, *Gleichheit*, 45.
55. Leibholz, *Gleichheit*, 57.

the prohibition of the substantial injustice of arbitrariness wherever relevant differences exist (*Willkürverbot*) within the circumstances of human life.[56] This relatedness of content (*Stoffbezogenheit*) between value-concepts and reality[57] is needed because 'the legal ideal is the concrete legal idea' of values.[58] The connection between ideal and value-idea is possible because of an intuitive sensual direct perception of *apriori* value through actually experienced objects. This delivers the standard for assessing the worthiness of empirical purposes.[59] Because for him, as it was for Aristotle, the content of justice within positive law is necessarily bound to communal life it is accessible through the legal instinct of this community.[60] Therefore this consciousness of law's content can be a reliable source for a legal order that an association of authority prescribes as valid for the conduct of human beings who feel committed to or, at a minimum, tolerate this order.[61] However, this law is an ought, not a will, that as purely empirical phenomenon of Being[62] can explain and identify the reason for the origin of law, the source, but cannot deliver conclusions as to the content of law.

In addition to the intuitively perceivable content of justice, which is expressed in the concepts of purpose and value of the positive law within a reality of a continuously moving and changing life,[63] there are also concepts of essence (*Wesensbegriffe*). Such concepts of essence are constructs of supra-temporal, unambiguous and unchangeable intellectual substances which can be detected only through a phenomenological substantive-intuitive analysis of essence.[64] They are foundational essences for ordering social life that determine the character of any constitution, such as state, democracy, government,

56. *Cf* Leibholz, *Gleichheit*, 67, 87–88.
57. Gerhard Leibholz, 'Begriffsbildung', 274–75.
58. Leibholz, *Gleichheit*, 59 (own translation).
59. Leibholz, *Gleichheit*, 59.
60. Leibholz, *Gleichheit*, 57, 61; Leibholz's position stands here in some similarity to Schmitt's for whom a decision is correct, that is, just, if another judge would have decided on the concrete case in the same way; Schmitt, *Gesetz und Urteil*, 68.
61. Leibholz, *Gleichheit*, 61–62, 65. The validity of legal norms includes the potentiality of enforceability, that is, the ability of influencing the factual behavior of human beings and states.
62. Leibholz, Begriffsbildung, 269.
63. *Cf* Leibholz, *Repräsentation und Gestaltwandel*, 105.
64. Leibholz, *Repräsentation und Gestaltwandel*, 88.

representation, sovereignty a. o.[65] Such epistemological essences of the theory of state (*staatstheoretische Wesenserkenntnisse*) can be recognised only subjectively and cannot be evidenced rationally. Within the legal science the rational, inductive method of the natural sciences is inapplicable for clarifying the relationship between idea and positive law because it presupposes the result. It is only useful for the application of already gained concepts.[66] Then, where the wording of a legal norm is inconclusive, the teleological method is suitable for determining content but finds its limits in the recognised essence (*Wesen*) of concepts.[67] This essential conceptual limit to the elastic adaptability of the written system of norms within the historic reality of life Leibholz states without further explanation. Even without being part of the codified text essences cannot be reversed in its content and are obligatory for positive law.[68]

For solving the legal question (*Rechtsfrage*) that is suspended between legal ideals and reality and for providing legal security, Leibholz rejects absolute theorems based on rational natural science. Defining "equality before the law" in reference to intuitively known justice permits him to prevent unjust arbitrariness and to acknowledge differences within the facts of life. Although absolutizing the changeability of the relative content of positive law he insists on supra-temporal, unambiguous essences within a constitutional order which are subjectively knowable to the conscience and can be evidenced in a synoptic phenomenological analysis.[69] In 1931 he adds that 'the legislator is not the only creator of law' because essences of

65. Leibholz, *Repräsentation und Gestaltwandel*, 18; Leibholz states that also outside of public law concepts of essence are present, such as contract, marriage, property, civil service, estates and others.
66. Leibholz, *Repräsentation und Gestaltwandel*, 14.
67. Leibholz, *Repräsentation und Gestaltwandel*, 16.
68. Leibholz, *Repräsentation und Gestaltwandel*, 106; Leibholz, 'Begriffsbildung', 273.
69. Although central to his 1929 thesis and of far-reaching consequence Leibholz dedicates to the methodological process of viewing essences (*Wesensschau*) only one sentence: 'Through a material-intuitive viewing in synoptic analysis the phenomenological-analytical consciousness has a tendency to make evident the essence of a Being that is grounded in an empirical form, the object, and to disclose thus at the same time the historically attached coincidences and to prove their extra-historical essential necessity.' Leibholz, *Repräsentation und Gestaltwandel*, 18 (own translation).

the theory of state are removed from any interpretation and rather 'flow from the nature of things, the essence of institutions and general perceptions of justice'.[70] For Leibholz there are absolute ideals outside the legal system as well as absolute essences beyond the written constitution. Positive concepts of law strive towards the ideals of law and are adaptable to the ever-changing facts of reality through applying the teleological method of interpretation. However, ideals flowing from the "nature of things" are intuitively knowable in difference to essences which are subjectively viewed (*Wesensschau*), but both are permanent, unchangeable substances. In 1932/33 he observes the incoming political regime's replacement of constitutional substance with a unitary consciousness that radically revises the 'constituted, metaphysical world of values of intellectual independent areas of life'.[71] He objects to the mystification of the theory of state and the demand of a politically 'correct faith' and observes that the state was not the only 'place of holiness'.[72] He rejects the reorientation of legal rights to state-centered legal conceptions that turn to "natural" forms of tradition. Instead he refers to a Germanist idea[73] of freedom, expressed in Gierke's 'inexhaustible German spirit of association',[74] and to the purpose of the individual's freedom of conscience that corresponds to a higher community of positive law (*Gesetz*).[75] This will ultimately determine the community's form-principle of being either a democracy or a dictatorship.[76]

---

70. Leibholz, ‚Begriffsbildung', 273.
71. Gerhard Leibholz, *Die Auflösung der liberalen Demokratie in Deutschland und das autoritäre Staatsbild* [The dissolution of liberal democracy in Germany and the authoritarian vision of the state], Wissenschaftliche Abhandlungen und Reden zur Philosophie, Politik und Geistesgeschichte XII (Munich: Duncker & Humblot, 1933), 55, 57, 70.
72. Leibholz, *Auflösung*, 74.
73. Leibholz included this reference to Germanist law in the January 1933 publication of his booklet *Die Auflösung der liberalen Demokratie in Deutschland und das autoritäre Staatsbild* most likely due to the fact that as the son of Jewish parents he found himself in a precarious situation within the developing political dynamics.
74. Gierke, *Genossenschaftsrecht*, 3.
75. *Cf* Leibholz, *Auflösung*, 60–61, 64–65, 73.
76. *Cf* Leibholz, *Auflösung*, 76.

Bonhoeffer's Theology in Relation to Leibholz' Jurisprudence

Bonhoeffer's discussion of the terms of written law (*Gesetz*), law (*Recht*), justice (*Gerechtigkeit*), but also the term judge (*Richter*) and their relation to love appears in two clusters of time-periods which are intersected by the March 1940 letter to Leibholz. The first concentration involves early studies on Aristotle's method, a redirection of the focus of "equality before the law",[77] a phenomenological discourse on the difference between theology and philosophy,[78] and his interpretation of Jesus' Sermon on the Mount.[79] In this period falls also Bonhoeffer's first public engagement on questions of law (*Recht*) and on church-state relations. Both are a direct response to the national-socialist racial legislation which affected Leibholz.[80] In assessing the Lutheran Church's self-understanding under the novel conditions set by the 1919 Weimar Constitution as 'Christ existing as church community'[81] Bonhoeffer's reference to the Aristotelian focus on community parallels Leibholz' s theory of state. But he differs from Leibholz insofar as he disputes the teleological character of this community towards a purpose[82] and instead defends the church-community as 'the objective work of the Spirit'.[83] In redirecting "equality before the law" to "equality before God" Bonhoeffer echoes Leibholz's demand of turning the only formal value of the basic rights of the Weimar Constitution into subjective legal claims of material value. Although without specifically mentioning Aristotle,[84] this connects to Bonhoeffer's previous study on Aristotle[85] insofar as it regards the consequences of the Aristotelian principle of self-evidence and the philosophical content for understanding theology as scientific

77. DBWE 1, *Sanctorum Communio.*
78. DBWE 2, *Act and Being.*
79. DBWE 4, *Discipleship.*
80. DBWE 12:285–97 and 361–73.
81. DBWE 1:121; this phrase that identifies the character of the church is repeated many times throughout the thesis.
82. DBWE 1:88.
83. DBWE 1:144.
84. Instead of discussing Aristotle Bonhoeffer discusses the 'absolute communist' idea of equality, equality in the orthodox understanding, as well as Georg Simmel's perspective; DBWE 1:204.
85. DBWE 9:202–8.

discipline,[86] and his rejection of logic as criteria while maintaining the Lutheran differentiation between the formal and the material side of issues. In the second period[87] Bonhoeffer not only summarises his theology concerning the rule of law and juristic terms but adds to his decisively Christ-centered perspective of the previous period a mature, if not radical, edge by going beyond method and including a discourse on the Roman law principle of *suum cuique*.

Prior to the Letter of March 1940

In his contribution to the Weimar controversy on method and direction Bonhoeffer criticises the scholastic demand for a methodological exact formal logical process of reasoning or for reality-conform, factual conceptual definitions.[88] He claims that in the structure of the laws of logic, according to concept, judgement, and conclusion, the ability to connect to the substance of truth and reality was lost. As if anticipating his later enduring theological pursuit, Bonhoeffer states that the Aristotelian question of the strained relation between logical truth and Christian self-evidenced knowledge remained,[89] despite attempts of solving it with claims to power and violations of logic. Rather reason and revelation are two independent sources of human knowledge in which the former connects to a natural theology that is knowable through observations of nature and human life while the latter denotes trans-rational divine mystery to which only *apriori* intuitive insight is possible[90] which remains outside the capacity of reason.[91] According to Bonhoeffer, despite the developments since Aristotle's time, through Reformation and until the contemporary age,[92] the various expressions of the relation of the separate spheres of

86. The interconnection and differences between theology and philosophy, between revelation and reason, in the twentieth century, became the subject matter of Bonhoeffer's *Habilitation* thesis *Act and Being*; DBWE 2.

87. DBWE 6, *Ethics*.

88. DBW 9: *Jugend und Studium 1918–1927* [The young Bonhoeffer 1918–1927], edited by Hans Pfeifer, in cooperation with Clifford Green and Carl-Jürgen Kaltenborn (Gütersloh: Kaiser / Gütersloher Verlagshaus, 1986) 328–29.

89. *Cf* DBW 9:331–32.

90. DBWE 9:306–7.

91. DBWE 9:306.

92. DBWE 8:316.

knowledge belong together, even though being variously expresses as *lex* and *evangelium*, *lex naturalis* and *lex moralis*, or law and gospel. Both can only be recognised in their relation to scripture, the 'highest *single* truth'.[93] However, the process of secularization has detached reason from scripture and has added the perspective of historicism's separation of time from revelation, of 'beginning' (potentiality) from 'completion' (reality).[94]

Despite the critique of Aristotelian reason Bonhoeffer agrees with Luther's distinction between formal and material evidence[95] and declares that "equality before the law" refers to a formal law (*Gesetz*) with only a value in itself that is void of the material content that the concept of equality demands. In Christian equality which places the human being in a formal way before God, the material equality recognises the 'concrete dissimilarity of all people'[96] which rests on the unequal particular circumstances of every person. In difference to modern philosophy of value which rejects absolute concepts Bonhoeffer insists that Christian equality has a universal aspect insofar as its formal side declares all human beings as sinners but provides at the same time an equal share in God's grace. The formal aspect of equality maintains the absolute distance between God and human beings and provides the options of obedience and disobedience[97] but is complimented by the material aspect that is 'based on the fact that *God is always the same*' (*der Gleiche*) which is proclaimed to the world in the cross's equal (*gleiche*) judgement and equal grace.[98] Affirming with Leibholz a material side to equality that recognises differences between human beings Bonhoeffer assigns an absolute aspect only to the formal side which permits for overcoming with God's equal-ness (*Gleichheit*) the distance between the formal and the material.

The differentiation between the formal and material which Bonhoeffer's theology has in common with jurisprudence remains a basic

93. DBWE 9:307–8; emphasis in original.

94. DBWE 1:143.

95. Bonhoeffer states in his critique of Aristotelian logic that Luther held fast to such formal thinking. He claimed that this is proven by Luther's request at the trial in Worms for presenting against his statements on scripture alternatively contradictory material evidence or formal illogical grounds; DBWE 9:303.

96. DBWE 1:206.

97. *Cf* DBWE 1:204–5.

98. DBWE 1:205 (emphasis in original).

notion. It reappears in a variety of different forms in his theology as it develops, such as in faith and redemption, in Adam and in Christ, in the cross and God's love, and it carries all of the law-related aspects until he finally unites both sides in the absoluteness of God's love and Jesus Christ as the Real One. In Bonhoeffer's theology the equally sinful human beings live in time, in history, since they had become separated from God through the Fall as it is told in scripture. Revelation enters this history in the form and fact of Jesus Christ in whom 'God's word became history'.[99] Expressed from a phenomenological perspective this means that only revelation can break the boundaries of the rational human being who otherwise remains enclosed in the ego and this-worldly circular thinking which is misperceived as of creative and original beginning.[100] But fallen, sinful humankind cannot venture with creative, philosophical reasoning or "reflexion" beyond God's *creatio ex nihilo* which belongs to God alone, describes the 'utterly unique'[101] primeval beginning, and is the absolute beginning of theology. With His love for His creation God in His grace redeems the human being who is stuck in the 'anxiety-causing middle'[102] of history's relativity. At the instance of utter subjectivity[103] and the moment of "nothingness" at the Christ-event on the cross, which was foreshadowed already at the Fall, Christ becomes through faith the new middle of human existence, history, and nature in the middle of the reality of time.[104] Reconciled to God through faith in the cross of Jesus Christ, God's love transforms in the history of this-worldly time the sinful human life 'in Adam'[105] into redeemed and reconciled human beings 'in Christ'.[106] In the middle of relative history God's absolute love is revealed to reason through faith in the redemptive and reconciling cross of Jesus Christ.

---

99. DBWE 1:143.
100. DBWE 2; also: DBWE 6:310–11. Humankind, neither knowing the end nor the beginning, but coming from the beginning and compelled to move to the end mistakes in an ultimate attempt at reflexion its philosophical thinking as the beginning of a creative nothingness; DBWE 3:28, 33.
101. DBWE 3:34
102. DBWE 3:30.
103. DBWE 6:128.
104. DBWE 12:324–27.
105. DBWE 2:136–50.
106. DBWE 2:150–61.

In homiletic exercises[107] and in the interpretation of the Sermon on the Mount which sets law (*Gesetz*) of the written commandments of the Decalogue and the gospel into relation,[108] Bonhoeffer appears to apply his objection to methodological logic while maintaining a differentiating formal and material structure in which the latter's substance is intrinsically perceived. Despite the antithetic character between law and gospel the latter is formally superior to the law while materially they are one in God's Word and Christ[109] because human beings are justified through faith due to Christ having fulfilled the law in his obedient suffering of the penalty for sin. Nonetheless, Bonhoeffer's formal approach of naming the Ten Commandments as God's initial claim on human beings, the subsequent judgement that the law is fulfilled, the following findings, and the concluding consequences of validity and application remains close to the previously criticised logical structure of concept, judgement, and conclusion. And it is noticeably similar to the established formal process regarding juristic judgements of stating the normative claim, pronouncing the judgement, stating reasoned findings, followed by the consequences of legal validity and enforcement.[110] Materially, though, in God's holy court (*Gericht*) of reconciliation the substance of injustice turns into justice based on His revelation in Christ.

In God's holy court the material content of law is not identical with God because this would dissolve God into the law for the purpose of establishing power over God and removing God as Lord over the law.[111] And justice, pronounced on the sinner through God's revealing self-evidence in Jesus' death on the cross, that is, in Jesus' complete submission to and understanding of God's will and law, averts the accusation that the cross demonstrates God's injustice. Rather by invoking the true law in complete personal communal unity with

107. DBWE 14:355–56; the homiletic exercises included sections of Galatians, but, at least as far as it is known, not an exercise on Gal 3:24 which Bonhoeffer mentions in his 1940 letter to Leibholz.

108. DBWE 14:335.

109. DBWE 14:336.

110. A general, coarse description of the legal process is as follows: *Anspruchsgrundlage* (legal basis for the claim), *Richterspruch* (Judge's decision), *Begründung* (jurisprudential grounds of the decision), *Rechtskraft* (legal validity), *Vollstreckung* (enforcement).

111. DBWE 4:117. See also DBWE 6:327.

God Jesus suffers because of the advocates of false law.[112] In his acceptance of the cross in communal unity with God and for the sake of the law Jesus "is" justice himself.[113] Participation in the new law of Christ's justice is granted in the real and simple obedience[114] of regular unassuming, hidden behavior of human beings of faith. This obedience is not marked by public good deeds or triumphant insistence on human freedom[115] but is the better justice if it remains invisible to the human being of faith. As invisible love obedience is not a human quality or visible habit or virtue[116] but a completely self-oblivious and unreflective act (*actus directus*),[117] a self-forgetting love bound solely to Christ. Love as act of simple obedience, love of Christ the Crucified, is love that has died to the old self but is found again by living in Christ[118] and for one's neighbors.

Beyond the Letter of March 1940

In the political context of the 1940s in which the letter to Leibholz was written Bonhoeffer adds with a discourse on the Roman law's *suum cuique* a partisan note to his theology regarding the material content of law. Justice remains subliminally a part of the discourse but the central focus turns to the secular world in which, despite God loving, judging and reconciling through Jesus, forms of law (*Gesetz*) have become the ultimate reality. In a context where legality has absorbed all legitimacy and all human being's individuality has disintegrated into worldly community led Bonhoeffer to address perpetual conflicts between mutually irreconcilable laws. Such laws are either being based on the Christian principle or on a worldly principle which turns the demand of obedience into violating either the one or the other law.[119] For reconciling this dilemma Bonhoeffer rejects ideology in favor of a responsibility that trusts in God's

112. DBWE 4:118.
113. DBWE 4:119.
114. DBWE 4:120, 150.
115. *Cf* DBWE 4: 147–48.
116. DBWE 4:151–52.
117. DBWE 4:152. Regarding Bonhoeffer's differentiation between *actus directus* (directness) and *actus reflexus* (reflection) see DBWE 2:28.
118. DBWE 4:152.
119. DBWE 6:264.

grace and holy court in which the reality of origin, essence, and goal is God in Jesus Christ.[120] Especially in cases where human existence is involved he calls on the essence of law (*Wesensgesetz*) and for an appropriateness to the subject matter (*Sachgemäßheit*) which both recall Leibholz's discourses on viewing essences (*Wesensschau*) and the relatedness of content (*Stoffbezogenheit*). Acknowledging that in the reality of this world legal systems are necessary to order communal life, he realises that whenever human existence is concerned in this reality nature or idea cannot sufficiently determine the material content of law. Then essence is located beyond any formal techniques of legal norms or the theory of state.[121] Actions within this reality must not only be appropriate but must also be done in selfless surrender of personal aspirations for the purpose of restoring the gift of Jesus Christ to the original relationship between the subject matter and the human beings.[122]

For Bonhoeffer, it is in God's court with God as judge (*Richter*) that the final judgement is pronounced in cases concerning human existence.[123] Then the ultimate reason (*ultima ratio*) is beyond the reason (*ratio*) of the law[124] of the relative order. For Bonhoeffer, formal procedures and legalities of statecraft do not exhaustively capture the essence of the law of the state. In the sphere of political necessities, which lays beyond regular legality, the appropriateness of an action is not determined by law (*Gesetz*) but through an appeal to the freedom of the acting human being.[125] But either way, for action within historic reality either based on law or on freedom in violation of law, the question of which law is the ultimate law must remain open because of its purely theoretical value. In either way the human being is guilty

120. DBWE 6:268–69, 270.

121. DBWE 6:271–72. For Bonhoeffer the theory of state and its laws include positivist legal orders and treaties, as well as all non-codified regulations and those forms of national and international political coexistence which are historically sanctioned, and finally the generally accepted moral principles of political life.

122. *Cf* DBWE 6:270–71.

123. DBW (Dietrich Bonhoeffer Werke) 6: *Ethik* [Ethics], edited by Ilse Tödt, Heinz Eduard Tödt, Ernst Feil and Clifford Green, 2nd edition (Gütersloh: Kaiser/Gütersloher Verlagshaus, 1998), 275: *Das Gericht bleibt bei Gott* (The court of justice remains with God.)

124. DBWE 6:273.

125. *Cf* DBWE 6:272–73.

and must live by divine grace and forgiveness.[126] In God's court is decisive only that the act was grounded in the love for human beings in the same way as Jesus, true to selfless love and despite being sinless, assumed the guilt of humanity.[127] This finding is not contradicted by the human conscience's call to a formal unity of the human being's self because materially conscience claims the autonomy of the ego, a position of *sicut deus*, which equates to a life 'in Adam' instead of living a life of faith 'in Christ' beyond the laws of the ego.[128]

The correct use of the freedom to act within history defines the rights (*Rechte*) of human existence because only in relations among human beings God's gift of natural life turns into rights. With God warranting such rights through the cross of Jesus they reflect God's glory in the midst of the fallen world and therefore are not claimable as human interests.[129] Whether the right to relative freedom, which differs from the faith-based God-gifted absolute freedom for God and the neighbor,[130] is correctly used or misused corresponds, according to Bonhoeffer, to the distinction between the "natural" and "unnatural", and calls to mind also Bonhoeffer's differentiation between living "in Adam" or "in Christ". Based on distinguishing between that which closes itself off and that which is directed toward Jesus Christ's coming,[131] Bonhoeffer defines the natural over against the unnatural as the form of life that God gifts and then preserves through justification, salvation, and renewal in Christ.[132] Thus "natural" is the God-gifted and preserved right to human existence among human relations within the relative reality of this world. The formal right to human existence among human relations is "natural" insofar as it is gifted and preserved by God. Determining the material content of this right leads Bonhoeffer into a discourse on the Roman principle of *suum cuique*.

Discussing Roman law in relation to God-given natural rights (*Rechte*) over against laws (*Gesetze*) which are set for a national socialist communal order Bonhoeffer defies the politically "correct

126. DBWE 6:274.
127. DBWE 6:275.
128. DBWE 6:276–78.
129. *Cf* DBWE 6:180.
130. DBWE 6:174.
131. DBWE 6:173.
132. DBWE 6:174, 176.

faith" of his contemporary time. For Bonhoeffer *suum cuique* is 'the highest possible recognition of reason' which corresponds to reality and observes the right that is gifted by God to every single human being within natural life.[133] By shortening the Roman principle of *suum cuique tribuere* (render to each the own) to the first two words Bonhoeffer prevents understanding the Roman phrase as regarding rights that can be distributed by human beings[134] and instead keeps the focus on God and on human life as an original *suum* in the sense of being gifted by God. To Bonhoeffer *suum cuique* is misunderstood if "the own" is replaced with "the same" (*Gleiche*). In that case, similar to Leibholz's assessment, the variety, dissimilarity, or multiplicity of the natural would be destroyed and would open the gate to subjective arbitrariness. To Bonhoeffer, "the own" recognises the priority of the rights that are objectively gifted with the natural over against abstract formal positive law. And although not specifically stating, by objecting to replacing "the own" with "the same" (*Gleiche*) Bonhoeffer rejects Leibholz's use of *suum cuique* because such an exchange of words would draw the Divine, the God who '*is always the same*'[135] (*der Gleiche*) into the sphere of human distribution and power.

However, when conflicts between rights within the natural, that is between mutually irreconcilable laws is concerned, *suum cuique*, despite being a paramount norm within worldly positive laws, is nonetheless set from outside of nature as divine law.[136] The essence of "giving each the own" captures the divine within the relative history if it searches within the limits of relative correctness for fulfilling all rights which Jesus Christ gifts through the Holy Spirit.[137] The essence (*Wesen*) of law, whether as rights (*Rechte*) or legislated law (*Gesetz*), find's its very own created and inborn law under Christ's rule in God's created, loved, and reconciled world. This essence is, according to Bonhoeffer, the reality of God's love for the world and for human beings.[138] The essence of this love of God is that 'God is love'. The biblical concept of the love that God self-reveals in Christ is that He alone is the foundation, the truth and the reality of love in which all

133. DBWE 6:184.
134. Reiner, 'Hauptgrundlagen', 3.
135. DBWE 1:205.
136. DBWE 6:181–82.
137. *Cf* DBWE 6:182–83.
138. *Cf* DBWE 16, 548, DBWE 6:394.

natural thought finds its origin and in which it participates.[139] It is not a human behavior or knowable law of nature but can be known only though knowing God's self-revelation in Jesus Christ, that is, in faith in his death at the cross.[140] The absolute essence of God's love for His creation, self-revealed in Jesus Christ's redeeming cross, appears in the reality of this world as God's mandates such as marriage, family, authority (*Obrigkeit*), church,[141] culture[142] etc.[143] They are communal structures that are not empowered and legitimised by history or worldly powers[144] but are assigned from above to remain until the end of the world.[145] They are expressions of God's absolute love and essence even though they may not be consciously perceived as such by human beings.[146]

Bonhoeffer's clarification that grounding worldly orders in Christ does not constitute the implementation of any foreign rule, such as a Jewish law,[147] appears as a pointed rejection of anti-Jewish political agitation. For Bonhoeffer, Christ liberates from foreign laws (*Gesetze*) and ideologies.[148] Thus God's incarnation does not serve a human ideal "law of nature" but liberates to genuine worldly reality.[149] Nonetheless, within the natural reality it is the task of reason to defend the right of every single person even if the divine background of God's creation and call to eternal life is not recognised.[150] Therefore where rights are endangered and defended within the relative it is not the single human being but God who defends the rights.[151] Thus those who use law (*Gesetz*) as the measure for judging other human beings

139. DBWE 6:335.
140. DBWE 6:334.
141. DBWE 6:55, DBWE 16:569.
142. DBWE 6:390.
143. Additionally, Bonhoeffer identifies as mandates the concepts of estate (*Stand*) and office (*Amt*), the latter in the sense of an administrative position, but only after they are cleansed and reclaimed from relative distortions; DBWE 6:390.
144. Humanly legitimised structures such as people, race, class, nation, society and others are dependent on factual circumstances of power and fluctuate with the orders of history; DBWE 6:69; DBWE 16:549.
145. DBWE 6:388–90.
146. *Cf* DBWE 6:70.
147. DBWE 16:547–48.
148. DBWE 16:550.
149. DBWE 16:548.
150. DBWE 6:184.
151. DBWE 6:185.

and see themselves as responsible for its implementation consider themselves above the law and forget that there is only one legislator and judge in the court of God.[152]

As announced in the 1940 letter, Bonhoeffer directs the legal question to be theologically understood as Christ not only being the mediator between God and the world but in the sense that he "is" God's revealing love within reality. Christ "is" the Real One.[153] His Christ-centered theology provides through faith in the fact of Christ's cross within the reality of historic time for human beings access to God's revelation of redemptive and reconciling love and a life that is "in Christ" beyond the sinfulness of Adam. In His absolute love for His creation God grants in His grace natural rights (*Rechte*), preserves life, and ensures final justice (*Gerechtigkeit*) over relative laws (*Gesetze*) and human justice, even though the relative law is needed for ordering communal life within the reality of this world. Thus, rights within historical reality are not abstract ideals but are because of their divine focus on justice 'pedagogic tools towards Christ'.[154] Proceeding from God being always the constant same (*der Gleiche*) ultimate justice remains in God's court (*Gericht*) and with God as judge (*Richter*). God's absolute justice is His love which is as essence directly, intuitively, perceivable by human beings and is manifested in absolute divine mandates for the purpose of ordering communal life within the relative time of history.

Reorienting "equality before the law" to "equality before God" lets Bonhoeffer draw a clear formal distinction between God's absolute law and justice on one side and rights within the reality of the relative world on the other side. Divinely gifted material content provides for human existence rights to natural life and relative freedom which are an expression of God's redeeming and reconciling love. This absolute essence of love is directly accessible through faith in God's revelation in Jesus Christ's cross and acted upon within the relative reality of this world and in direct obedience which is unknowingly directed towards the Divine. For Leibholz rights are part of the legal system of laws within history which is directed towards an absolute legal ideal that is intuitively known by the human being. Furthermore, the legal

152. DBWE 6:327–28.
153. DBWE 6:261–63.
154. DBWE 15:302.

system, and in particular a constitution, contains absolute essences which can be viewed rationally through method. The "test case" for the difference between absolute divine law and absolute human law is for Bonhoeffer the subject matter of human existence in which the divinely created natural law provides essence to human law. In this discussion Bonhoeffer radicalises his argument through discussing Roman law which Leibholz avoids. Rights within human legal systems are for Bonhoeffer not based on laws of nature in a scientific sense but in the divinely revealed essence of absolute love which directly opposes Leibholz's understanding of law and legal systems in the sense of jurisprudence as science and his rejection of natural law. While for Leibholz within the legal system the legal value of rights must relate to the circumstances of reality, so similarly also for Bonhoeffer essence and actions within reality must stand in an appropriate relation. Both recognise essences that are immutable and absolute but for Leibholz they are essences that are attached to and are underlying the constitution while for Bonhoeffer they are mandates provided by God within history. Finally, for both the sphere of politics remains beyond the legal system and human made law but for Bonhoeffer it rests nonetheless "before God". Overall, Leibholz answers the legal question with an intuitively known legal ideal and viewing of essence. Bonhoeffer closes the legal question with direct obedience to God's love, His mandates, and His self-revelation in Christ.

Conclusion

In 1967 the jurist Ernst-Wolfgang Böckenförde, a close post-war friend and student of Carl Schmitt, caused a disturbance within German jurisprudence and politics by declaring that the liberal, secular state depends on preconditions that cannot be guaranteed by the state itself.[155] He questions whether values or natural moral or Christianity provide the internal bond between human beings of a state-community who otherwise are each left in their freedom to depend on their self.[156] Without advocating a return to the "Christian" state of the nineteenth century he recognises the risk the state takes especially in

155. Ernst-Wolfgang Böckenförde, *Recht, Staat, Freiheit* [Law, state, freedom], 2nd extended edition (Frankfurt am Main: Suhrkamp, 2006), 112.

156. Böckenförde, *Recht, Staat Freiheit*, 111.

times of crisis and advocates that Christians instead of understanding their state's secularity as something foreign should rather recognise it as a chance to freedom which is theirs to support and realise.[157] At the time of Böckenförde's statement post-war Germany had returned with the 1949 Basic Law to a positivist constitutional system[158] which, however, named God in its preamble as an underlying motivation; a reference which Leibholz supported.[159] As Leibholz had argued in the 1920s, the basic rights that had been only programmatically listed in the Weimar Constitution became in the Basic Law claimable subjective rights, and a Federal Constitutional Court had been installed as 'the ultimate juristic authority of the state'.[160] At the 1951 inaugural formation of this Court, which is meant to provide judicial oversight to governmental and legislative institutions of the democratic republic, Leibholz was called as one of its first judges.[161]

Having been familiar with Bonhoeffer's essays in *Ethics*[162] and having abandoned subsequent to the 1940 letter during his years of exile in England his 1920s refusal of discussing 'the uncountable theological, jurisprudential, or ethical attempts for defining the concept of justice',[163] Böckenförde's statement might not have come as a great surprise to Leibholz. Thus, in 1942, Leibholz had stated that the 'rule of pure love' is 'relevant to man's conduct' in the reality of this world in which the rules of the Sermon on the Mount need 'to be put into daily practice'.[164] Reason and moral philosophy, he stated, were no longer delivering universally acceptable standards for a concept of justice.[165] Concluding from the contemporary experience that it was not possible to build a democracy on a secular basis alone[166] boundaries for political authorities needed to be drawn from the Christian

157. Böckenförde, *Recht, Staat, Freiheit*, 112–13.
158. Stolleis, 'Legitimation', 54.
159. Wiegandt, *Norm und Wirklickeit*, 253.
160. Michael Stolleis, 'The profile of the judge in the European tradition', in *A Journal of the Humanities and Social Sciences* (TRAMES) 12 (62/57)/2 (2008): 211.
161. Gerhard Leibholz, 'The Federal Constitutional Court in the Constitutional System of the Federal Republic of Germany' (1963), in *Politics and Law*, 271–85.
162. The first version of Bonhoeffer's *Ethics* was published in 1949 in the German language.
163. Leibholz, *Gleichheit*, 58 (own translation).
164. Gerhard Leibholz, 'Christianity, Politics, and Power', in *Politics and Law*, 93.
165. Leibholz, 'Foundations', 255.
166. Wiegandt, *Norm und Wirklickeit*, 252.

natural law for the purpose of preventing to fill the idea of justice with arbitrary content and political decisionism.[167] The demise of the Weimar democracy he assessed as having rested on a wrongly conceived limitless freedom which even had made possible the self-abolition of the Constitution instead of protecting its substance[168] and he demanded freedom to be bound by the existential foundations which make a liberal democracy functionally possible.[169] And in 1969 in remembrance of the failed 1944 coup d'état in which Bonhoeffer and other relatives had been involved, he referred directly to the Christian faith for asserting rights to life and freedom beyond the state that may even permit the removal of a despotic regime.[170]

Nevertheless, Leibholz never again engaged in discourses regarding legal theory, methodological questions, or criticism leveled against his judgements, especially when references to constitutional essences were involved.[171] Even though he continued to uphold his thesis of concepts of essence that are foundational to the constitution (representation, sovereignty, democracy, state etc.) and social life (property, marriage, etc) he never attempted to clarify his phenomenological method but instead he forthwith only delivered the results of his analysis.[172] Thus as a judge at the Federal Constitutional

---

167. Gerhard Leibholz, 'Politics and Natural Law', in *Politics and Law*, 21.
168. Already during the late Weimar Republic Leibholz had agreed with the teaching of the untouchability of the constitution's central substance which had been developed by Carl Schmitt, *Constitutional Theory*, translated by Jeffrey Seitzer (Durham: Duke University Press, 2008), originally published in 1928 as *Verfassungslehre* by Duncker & Humblot (Munich); Wiegandt, *Norm und Wirklickeit*, 267.
169. Wiegandt, *Norm und Wirklickeit*, 265–66.
170. Gerhard Leibholz, 'Der Gestaltwandel der Demokratie im 20. Jahrhundert' [The changes in the form of democracy in the 20th century], in *Repräsentation und Gestaltwandel*, 212; see also same, 'Das Vermächtnis des 20. Juli 1944' [The legacy of 20 July 1944] (1969), in *Festschrift für Gebhard Müller: Zum 70. Geburtstag des Präsidenten des Bundesverfassungsgerichts* [In honor of Gebhard *Müller: To the 70th birthday of the president of the* Federal Constitutional Court], edited by Theo Ritterspach and Willi Geiher, 185-95 (Tübingen: 1970), 188.
171. Wiegandt, *Norm und Wirklickeit*, 79, 297, 304.
172. Wiegandt, *Norm und Wirklickeit*, 95.

Court he delivered in several cases[173] interpretations without reasoned justifications as to the stated essence. His first step of the cognition of essence (*Wesenserkenntnis*) leads straight into the second step of depicting almost any arbitrary position as self-evidently correct and is underlined with phrases such as 'according to essence and nature',[174] '*apriori* concept of law' (*Rechtsbegriffe*), or 'the essence and structure of phenomena immanent to the constitution'.[175] Thus in the last consequence such essences remain subjective evaluations.[176] For these he has been criticised of being extremely close to the Dezisonism of his mentor of the 1920s, Carl Schmitt,[177] who advocated arbitrary sovereign freedom.[178] However, Leibholz's method of moving from a presupposed absolute legal concept to a wished for legal formation may be excused with pointing to a practicability that attempts to capture from a teleological perspective the political and social reality in a static positivist law without losing the law's character (*Recht*) that is focused towards a legal ideal. In a self-assessment Leibholz locates himself between natural law and sociological positivism.[179] And despite his decade-long interchanges with Bonhoeffer's theology Leibholz may have refrained from any religious faith statements due

173. One of the cases concerned the tension between the principle of representation and the principle of the party-state (article 21 and article 38 Basic Law of the Federal Republic of Germany); for a discussion of this case see Wiegandt, 218, 301–2. In another case the criteria for a juristic definition of an "organ" of the constitution and the definition's consequences for the overall understanding of the constitution was at stake. According to Leibholz 'organs of the constitution' are institutions that are in their essence unequivocally determined in their content and from which flow in intellectual necessity specific legal consequences from which even the legislator cannot deviate; a discussion of this case can be found in Wiegandt, *Norm und Wirklickeit*, 296–97, 301.
174. Gerhard Leibholz, '"Status"-Frage', in *Journal des öffentlichen Rechts (JöR)* N.F. 6 (1957): 131.
175. Gerhard Leibholz, 'Bemerkungen'[Remarks], in *Journal des öffentlichen Rechts (JöR)* N.F. 6 (1957): 195–96.
176. Wiegandt, *Norm und Wirklickeit*, 301.
177. Radler, 'The Leibholz—Schmitt connection', 684–88.
178. Wiegandt, *Norm und Wirklickeit*, 300, 304, 308.
179. Gerhard Leibholz, 'Verfassungsrecht und Verfassungswirklichkeit' [Constitutional law and constitutional reality] (1955), in *Strukturprobleme der modernen Demokratie*, 277–81.

to the basic constitutional right of religious freedom[180] and of being conscious that in his position as judge he was called to uphold the right's essence not only in regards to Christianity.

The legal question that Schmitt had posted in 1912 as to what contributes to decisions which are located between law and judgment in a way that it can provide security in the reality of this world and which Böckenförde has updated in asking for an internal bond between the freedom of human beings and political contextual reality has not yet been completely answered. In the search of our contemporary time for an integrating justice in which populist-autocratic ideas compete for the meaning of law and justice with the democratic theory of state's need for trust in the rule of law, Bonhoeffer's interaction with Leibholz continues to provide valuable insights for relating absolutes to the relative reality of this world.

180. Article 4, para 1 and 2; Article 3, para 3 Basic Law of the Federal Republic of Germany.

Book Review

John A Moses:

Anglicanism: Catholic Evangelical or Evangelical Catholic? Essays Ecumenical and Polemical. Homage to Dietrich Bonhoeffer, Hans Küng, Martin Luther and John Henry Newman.

ATF Adelaide, 2019. xxxiii + 155.

The leading concerns of this book are closely connected with the author's life. The first is the focused discourse around Catholic/Evangelical ecclesial identity and authority. The second and no less significant is the religious formation of John Moses, his training and work as an academic historian and his churchly service, theologically and as a priest. His introducing himself and his formative stages of his career, which are clearly integral to his outlook is a real plus, and his 'historiographical voice' persists across the churchly chapters that follow.

The book also embodies a *third* dimension, which shows up on its somewhat crowded title-page with its 'homage' listing of four significant figures of post-medieval church history, from Luther to the present. Of these named 'outsiders' only one, Cardinal Newman, was an Anglican, who then famously converted to Rome in 1845. It is therewith obvious that the great subject of this volume is too important not to include strong voices beyond those of the writer and his own Communion. That Bonhoeffer is given pride of place will not surprise readers of Moses' significant 2009 volume on the man: *Reluctant Revolutionary*. Significant Anglicans, beginning with Richard Hooker, are not underrepresented. Moreover, they include a fair number of Australians, Felix Arnott, Peter Carnley, Philip Freier among others. Moreover, a special chapter is devoted to the uniquely talented theologian (and mid-century editor of the acclaimed *Australian Church Quarterly*), Fr. Peter Bennie.

The Sydney harbour bridge and '*Eternity*' feature on the book's colourful front cover, an allusion to Sydney Anglicans' most beloved character, Arthur Stace, who anonymously etched 'Eternity' on the streets of Sydney for 35 years. In contrast to this charming declaration of faith, Moses' Table of Contents refers to complex lived realities, to paradox, paradigms and problems. Readers might be taken aback somewhat by the first chapter heading: 'The Chaos of Anglicanism'. 'Sydney-type Anglicanism', it emerges, is a deeply worrying, seemingly intractable and self-defeating issue in Anglicanism and the wider context of Australia's ascendant secular culture. Moses writes:

> The insistence of fundamentalist or so-called Bible Christians on enforcing an uncompromisingly literal interpretation of Holy Scripture . . . has led to a totally avoidable polarisation within Anglicanism that has crippled its capacity to witness to a world in dire need of the healing message of the Gospel. (p 59)

The author does not step away from noting 'a chilling resemblance to *fascism*', and to what he perceives as tragic 'one party control'. He is equally abnegating of papalist infallibility dogma.

It is in view of this situation that Moses presents a vigorous defence of 'traditional Prayer Book Anglicanism'; and he invokes the honoured cause of Church unity, for the support of which the Anglican Communion is seen as ideally positioned between the Protestant Churches and Catholicism—with 'a clear vocation to be the means of reconciliation within the divided Body of Christ' (p 84). Accordingly, the requirement that the Bible be read as the 'inerrant' and 'propositional word of God', as supported by the late Canadian theologian, James I. Packer (1926–2020), is rejected by the central essays of the book. Such interpretive legalism must result, so the author maintains, in forms of 'cognitive dissonance' and in disharmony and confusion among Christians of our day. And it leads, furthermore, to the deconstruction of liturgical worship and to 'church planting' with little regard to existing ecclesial order.

Though the present volume thus confronts the untoward trends and negative developments, it rises up from a great wealth, namely, the supple Anglican tradition and its historic ecumenical legacy. This happens here not at arms' length but courtesy of the productive scholarship and undeniable ministerial experience of the author and his helpers.

This volume would place its readers where theology and the Church in the world meet. 'A fortress mentality has no place in Christianity', Moses emphasises. The central chapters impel discussion of hugely consequential—if controverted—realities. Such substantial issues have to do with the Bible, with Church authority, Evangelicalism, and ethics, to name the more prominent. The author himself pens and here publishes two sets of 'Theses' that call for focused discussion and scrutiny.

And again *other* voices are made audible and available, such as:

1. A discussion on the question of freedom in terms of the *New Testament* will include weighing Queensland scholar Michael Lattke's ten theses (here reprinted in full, pp 110–113);
2. The *Evangelicalism* debate is bound to benefit if one takes account of the work of Piggin and Linder on *Evangelical Christians in Australian History*, which Moses reviews in an appendix;
3. How *authority* in the Anglican Communion (involving biblical, traditional and rational components) is treated, appears in a further appended paper by former Primate, Archbishop Keith Rayner;
4. Issues of *ethics* bring Bonhoeffer and his witness to 'the man for others' into play (pp 26–29). It is in the context of the Lutheran pastor's costly opposition to Third Reich oppression, that John Moses' criticism of 'what might be called "official government racism" in our society' finds forthright expression:

> . . . our treatment of Aborigines both historically and currently together with the handling of the refugee question challenges our national commitment to the ethics of the New Testament that should be the foundation of our political culture.

(Inadvertently and despite frequent references in the text Bonhoeffer's name is missing from the Index).

Anglicanism: Catholic Evangelical or Evangelical Catholic? is a critical but positive and even optimistic contribution to 'comparative symbolics' studies. Ecumenical hopes are alive and are shaping reality. Homage is paid to the Wittenberg reformer in connection with 'what is called "the Lutheran Agenda"'. And productive inter-church dialogue may well be further stimulated by the assertion that, when it comes to the crucial issue of justification by faith, 'Anglicans have always been Lutherans as well as Catholics . . .' But thankfully this is said in the purview of even broader ecumenical concord being already attained, the deepest divide since the Reformation [over justification by faith] having been bridged in the Roman Catholic-Lutheran agreements culminating in the Augsburg joint statement of 1999. '[A]n entirely new context' has arrived. And: 'Justification is not a heretical "Protestant" teaching; it is anchored four-square in the New Testament, and what is in the New Testament is completely Catholic'.

Maurice Schild
Emeritus Lecturer of Church History
Australian Lutheran College
MCD University of Divinity, Adelaide, Australia

Contributors

Dr Rachael Kohn AO FRSN, has taught Religious Studies in Canada, Britain and Australia. After teaching Religious Studies at the University of Sydney (1988–92), she joined the Australian Broadcasting Corporation producing and presenting programs on religion, including Religion Report, Religion Today, The Ark, and the long running The Spirit of Things from 1997–2018). She has authored numerous articles, chapters and two books, *The New Believers: Reimagining God* (2004) and *Curious Obsessions in the History of Science and Spirituality* (2007/2020). She is on the editorial board of *The Bonhoeffer Legacy: An International Journal.*

Rev Dr Charles Ringma has taught in universities, seminaries, and colleges in Australia, New Zealand, South East Asia, and Canada. He is Emeritus Professor, Regent College, University of British Columbia, Vancouver, an Honorary Research Associate Professor at University of Queensland, Australia and Adjunct Faculty at Asian Theological Seminary, Philippines. He is a Franciscan Tertiary (*tssf*), works for social justice and plants rain forest trees. Ringma has authored many books including *Seize the Day with Dietrich Bonhoeffer*. He lives in Brisbane, Australia.

Dr Michael (Mick) Duncan is Adjunct Lecturer in Applied Theology, with a focus on NZ society, Urban Mission and Cross-Cultural Studies at Carey Baptist College in Auckland, New Zealand. He is also lecturer at Stirling College Melbourne and Creation Care Study Program (US). He is Chair of Open Homes Foundation and on the Board of World Vision. His books include: *Move Out* (1984), *Costly Mis-*

sion (1996), *Wild Ones* (2006), *Alongsiders* (2013), *Who Stands Fast* (2014). His research Masters degree explored 'A Theological Ethic of Initiative' from the life of Dietrich Bonhoeffer.'

Rabbi Dr Martin Lockshin is University Professor Emeritus of Humanities and Hebrew at York University. His work centres on the great medieval Bible commentators, particularly Rabbi Samuel ben Meir (Rashbam), and has translated his commentary on Leviticus and Numbers into English (2001). His explanations of Rashbam's comments on the Pentateuch form the bulk of his English volumes (Rabbi Samuel ben Meir's Commentary on Genesis, Exodus, Leviticus, Numbers and Deuteronomy) and of his Hebrew volumes (Peirush ha Rashbam al ha-Torah). Lockshin holds a PhD from Brandeis University and rabbinical ordination from Yeshivat Mercaz Harav Kook in Israel. He lives in Jerusalem.

Assistant Professor Alex Green is Director of Undergraduate Studies in the Department of Jewish Thought at the University of Buffalo (SUNY). He received his MA in Jewish Thought at Hebrew University and PhD at the Department for the Study of Religion at the University of Toronto. His research focuses on medieval Jewish philosophy, ethics and the history of biblical interpretation. His books are *The Virtue of Levi Gersonides* (Palgrave 2016) and *Power and Progress: Joseph ibn Kaspi and the Meaning of History* (SUNY Press 2019).

Professor Dominic Johnson holds the Alastair Buchan Chair of International Relations at Oxford University and is Co-Director of the Oxford Martin School 'Natural Governance Program'. Johnson received his DPhil from Oxford University in evolutionary biology and a PhD from Geneva University in political science. He has written several books including *Strategic Instincts: The Adaptive Advantages of Cognitive Biases in International Politics* (Princeton University Press 2020) and *God is Watching You: How the Fear of God Makes Us Human* (OUP 2015).

Professor Joseph Bulbulia is Professor of Psychology in the Faculty of Science at Victoria University of Wellington (2020 to present) and formerly held the Maclaurin Goodfellow Chair in the school of Humanities, Faculty of Arts at the University of Auckland (2018–20).

He is co-editor of the *Religion, Brain & Behavior* online journal and is on the Senior Management Team of the New Zealand Attitudes and Values Study (tracking 15,000 people each year for 20 years). He is past President of the International Association for the Cognitive Science of Religion.

Dr. Karola Radler is Postdoctoral Research Fellow: Theology and Jurisprudence and Research Associate in Systematic Theology, Faculty of Theology, Stellenbosch University, SA. She is also Associate Teaching Faculty, St. Stephen's College at University of Alberta, Edmonton, Canada.

Dr Maurice Schild is Emeritus Lecturer at the Australian Lutheran College, Adelaide, where he taught church history from 1970–2000. He has written numerous articles in English and German, and authored *The Lutherans in Australia: Religious Community Profiles*, edited by PH Hughes (Canberra: Australian Government Publishing, 1996). Schild is on the Editorial Board of *The Bonhoeffer Legacy: an International Journal.*

www.ingramcontent.com/pod-product-compliance
Lightning Source LLC
Jackson TN
JSHW020001180426
101046JS00006B/192
9781922582430